/ – /

WHY TEACHERS FAIL

JOHN M. LEMBO
Millersville State College

Charles E. Merrill Publishing Co.
A Bell & Howell Company
Columbus, Ohio

Standard book number: 0–675–09269–8

Library of Congress Catalog Card Number: 73–1333503

2 3 4 5 6 7 8 9 0 – 75 74 73 72 71

Printed in the United States of America

PREFACE

My purpose in writing *Why Teachers Fail* is twofold. First, I wish to discuss critically some of the teaching policies and practices that prevent students from learning in reasonably satisfying ways. The first four chapters are devoted to this end. Second, I wish to advance some recommendations for improving the kind of teaching and learning that takes place in the schools. These recommendations are presented in Chapters 5, 6, 7 and 8.

The intent of this book is to encourage constructive argument, discussion and debate about some of the basic issues which face teachers and the schools and to provoke constructive change in the kind of teaching that takes place in the classroom. It is neither a definitive analysis of the current educational scene nor a blueprint for total educational reform.

Neither the title nor the content of this book should be interpreted to mean that *teachers* alone are to blame when students do not profit from schooling in satisfying ways. There are a number of conditions, both inside our public schools and in our teacher training institutions, which make it exceedingly difficult for many of our teachers to develop constructive kinds of teaching strategies. Also, not *all* of our teachers are failures. There are many remarkably competent teachers in our public schools. Unfortunately, they do not constitute the majority.

Why Teachers Fail has not been written for educators only. I hope to convey to all people concerned about education that fundamental changes need to take place in the schooling process if the individual student is to help solve, rather than add to, the complex economic, political and social problems that go unresolved day after day.

I wish to thank all of the people who have been helpful in the preparation of this book. The comments and suggestions made by Kris Evans, Evelyn Stevens, and Richard Olds have been especially valuable. I wish to express a special note of appreciation to Gail Palmer of Charles E. Merrill Publishing Company for her editorial assistance. Finally, I am deeply indebted to my wife, Judy, who typed and copy read the manuscript and provided me with encouragement and support during its writing.

CONTENTS

WHY TEACHERS FAIL

1

THE PROBLEM

INDICATIONS OF FAILURE

There are a number of indications that the schools are not shaping the development of students in ways that are satisfactory to students and society. What are these indications?

Overt Dropouts

Each year nearly one million youths drop out of school before completing their twelve years of basic education. (46) Nearly one-third of these dropouts do not go beyond the eighth grade. Looking at school after school in most of our cities we find that one-third to one-half of the students at each age level fail to complete high school. (38)

Nonpromotion

Added to the high rate of dropouts are the large numbers of students who each year are not promoted; they are retained even though most of them will show *no* improvement in their academic work after repeating the grade. (12, 22) Frequently, in fact, they regress in the overall performance levels they achieve. Many children (some of whom are promoted) show gradual declines in their I.Q.'s as they attempt to progress through school. (38) The behavior of a student who slips further and further

OF FAILURE

behind each year is quite predictable; he comes to believe that he is basically unsuited for academic work, and he begins to view the school as an impossible place in which to acquire useful skills. (50) Like the dropout, he seeks accomplishment and recognition outside the educational system. The picture in higher education is not much different. Many studies indicate that on the average 50 per cent of the students who enter four-year college degree programs fail to complete them. (2) At some institutions the attrition rate is higher. About 20 per cent of the individuals over 25 years of age in the United States have attended college, but only about 10 per cent have earned one or more degrees.

Stay-in Dropouts

Although most students remain in school, i.e., they are physically present, many of these students drop out of the schooling process psychologically. These particular students do not fail in the traditional manner for they manage to achieve passing grades. However, they are failures in the sense that they do not find school experiences relevant to their lives. Many students feel that the bulk of their school experiences are part of a total educational process that is largely artificial, contrived and devoid of real meaning. For example, the knowledge and skills acquired in civics are viewed by many students as virtually useless when dealing with the

3

real power structure in a community. Another example is high school history, which, as Friedenberg suggests, "is not even propaganda, because nobody is expected to believe it or to be moved by it; it is received as official myth." (9, p. 13) Consequently, many students take the line of least resistance by conforming to the expectations of their culture— waiting out the number of years they need to receive their passports to college and/or a job.

Poorly-Prepared Successes

Although many students are viewed as successful because they have made it through the current educational system with flying colors, i.e., they have completed more than the minimum course requirements and have received excellent grades, many of these students have developed little concern for or understanding of the problems of man and society. For example, many students perform well in terms of their understanding of factual materials and concepts in a Problems of Democracy class, yet oppose integrated schools. One study (41), which examined the political and social beliefs of teenagers, disclosed that 51 per cent of the high school students sampled disagreed with the desirability of having freedom of the press. Forty-two per cent agreed with the researcher's statement that the police may use physical or psychological torture ("the third degree") to make a man talk, despite Article V of the Bill of Rights: ". . . nor shall [he] be compelled in any criminal case to be witness against himself."

Many students receive high grades during their stay in school yet are appallingly ignorant of some of the most basic issues and problems that confront man. Fantini and Weinstein point out that large numbers of academically successful students leave the schools poorly prepared to function in constructive and reasonably satisfying ways.

> The middle class children who succeed in school . . . can pass the tests and get promoted. But have they been really prepared for adult life? The divorce rate, the incidence of ulcers and other psychosomatic illnesses, the vast sums spent each year on psychotherapy, indicate that they have not. The rigidity with which political parties are adhered to without respect to issues is another symptom, as is the startlingly low percentage of the population that votes even in presidential elections. (6, p. 143)

Cheating

Students' poor levels of meaningful learning are not the only behaviors which indicate that all is not well with the schools. Many students exhibit undesirable kinds of moral and emotional behavior. Cheating, for example, is widespread among the academically successful and unsuccessful alike; many students cheat even though they would receive good grades without cheating. (48) Bowers reports, from a study of over 5,000 students at 99 colleges and universities, that approximately 50 per cent of the students have cheated at some time in their college work. It is estimated that as high as 25 per cent of high achievers were involved in cheating at some time in their college careers. (1)

Drugs

The increased use of illicit drugs among school age individuals is another indication that today's youngsters are not developing in socially construc-tive ways. "An estimated one-third to one-half of the U.S.'s 14.5 million high school students have tried a variety of drugs, and the number of users is steadily rising." (36, p. 65) At the college level, the proportion of users is also unsettling; at some colleges at least 75 per cent of the student body uses marijuana. (35) The use of more dangerous drugs, such as LSD, is of even greater concern. It is estimated that 10,000 or more students have used LSD at the University of California alone. (34)

Psychiatric Help

There is evidence that the proportion of school age persons seeking psy-chiatric assistance is increasing sharply. At the college level some evi-dence suggests that one out of five students needs psychiatric help during his four years at college. (49) (It is important to note that only half of these students are likely to receive this help.) Psychiatric and counseling centers at virtually all colleges and universities report sharp increases in the percentage of services which they have provided students over the last few years. At Massachusetts Institute of Technology, psychiatric help to students has increased nearly 50 per cent over a three-year period. (21)

Suicide

Another indication that the young are not profiting from school in the desired ways is the rising rate of suicide among children and adolescents. Some data indicate that in recent years (1950 to 1960) the incidence of suicide for both male and female youths has approximately doubled. (15) Among college students, death by suicide is second only to acci-dents as the major cause of death. (33) There is evidence to suggest that most school age youngsters who commit suicide have normal or superior intelligences, yet perform poorly in school. (15, 33)

Inner-City Riots

The "Riot Report" of the President's Commission, published in 1968, described the typical rioter as between 15 and 24 years of age and a *high school dropout.* (42) To the President's Commission this dropout status was "the most dramatic evidence of the relationship between educational practices and civil disorder." (42, p. 425) Kenneth B. Clark (23) feels strongly about the relationship between public education and inner-city violence, maintaining that "the public schools are criminally inefficient" and that they are "spawning hundreds of thousands of functional illiterates" who are the "combustibles" in our cities. "Riots in our inner cities . . . are directly related to the flagrant ineffectiveness of our public schools." (23, p. 57)

To summarize, the schools are expected to produce young people who think, feel and value as creative and productive individuals, who have a sense of personal worth, who are concerned about the plight of man, and who have an anticipation about the future and a belief that they have a place in it. Yet in practice, the schools are not producing young people who behave in these ways. Many youths, some who suffer from disabling handicaps and others who have special talents which place them apart from their peers, receive no special attention to their unique needs in the schools. Even students who appear to be "adjusting" well to the educational system often do not demonstrate knowledge, skills, and values which are socially constructive. The incidences of nonpromotion, dropout, poorly-prepared successes, alienation, need for psychiatric help and inner-city riots make it quite clear that millions of children and adolescents are not adequately developing the skills to read, to reason logically, and to deal with the personal and social issues and problems they face. The lack of "fit" between the conditions which the schools now provide and the needs of our young people is so obvious and widespread that one can safely say that today's schools do not promote the learning and development of even half our youths in reasonably satisfying ways. (13) The conclusion is unmistakable: *Failure of the young to profit from schooling in ways which are constructive and of value to themselves and society is our most serious educational problem.*

CAUSES OF FAILURE

To be sure, there are many out-of-school conditions, e.g., family and social, which have a corrosive effect on the learning and development processes of children. Schools can choose to ignore these influences, scapegoat the family and society, or come to grips with the conditions they find. If the schools choose to ignore or scapegoat these influences for the problems they present, the schools must accept no small part of the blame when students perform poorly. Students' restricted backgrounds cannot be held accountable for inadequate teaching. This variable is irrelevant in providing optimum learning conditions *within* the classroom. It is unfortunate that in recent years the concern for equality of opportunity and the rapid growth in educational technology, enrollment, and administrative procedures for operating institutions have drawn attention away from the classroom teacher as the director of learning. However, unless the classroom teacher's policies and practices are viewed as the most significant conditions in determining the direction and quality of classroom learning and unless attempts at improving classroom learning focus on the formulation of more effective teaching policies and practices, there will be no significant reduction in the number of students who year after year become alienated from the educational process and live each day with the belief that they are "nobody" and are going "no place." *The basic supposition I am advancing is that while there are many complex factors, physical, psychological, economic and sociological, which account for each child's school performance, the basic cause of failure is the schooling process itself. Students do not enter school as failures; when students "fail," it is the practices which teachers and administrators individually and collectively employ that are at fault.*

What are among the most destructive practices found in the schools? They are (a) the employment of a predetermined set of learning conditions to manipulate each student's learning, (b) an emphasis on subject matter, materials and learning approaches which are irrelevant to students' lives and (c) an unwillingness to value students' concerns and personal needs over the processes of competition and administrative efficiency. Let us turn to the first of these influences, the teacher's practice of imposing predetermined learning conditions on each student.

2

PREDETERMINED

Every teacher has his own beliefs about why students perform and behave as they do and what good teaching is. His private beliefs in turn serve as the basis for employing particular kinds of practices in the classroom. It may be inferred from the foregoing that a major cause of school failure is to be found in the unwarranted assumptions about human learning and development that teachers hold, and in their consequent teaching practices.

Perhaps the most widely held belief about human learning and development and one on which many indefensible educational policies and practices are based, is that *without a predetermined set of conditions, students will not learn and develop in a manner that is constructive and of value to themselves and society.* This belief is based on four erroneous assumptions: first, careful manipulation is needed for students to learn; second, adults know best what students ought to learn; third, there is a particular process of learning through which all students should be guided; and fourth, there is a particular level of learning and performance that all students need to achieve. But, is careful manipulation needed for students to learn and develop in constructive ways?

CAREFUL MANIPULATION

The kind and amount of freedom students should be given is a much debated issue, and there is considerable confusion about the meaning

LEARNING CONDITIONS

of guidance. Educators often fail to distinguish between *imposing a pre-determined set of learning conditions* on a student, and *designing conditions that are most appropriate* for him to learn.

The first view assumes that students need to be *made* to learn, that unless young people are pressed into particular behavior patterns they will not develop in ways that are advantageous to themselves and others. In contrast with this view is the belief that an individual has inherent in him a basic thrust to explore, to know, to find meaning in reality, and to develop the performance capabilities needed to be competent in dealing with his environment. Youths do not need to be coerced to learn and develop in constructive ways. When each individual is valued for *himself,* and when assistance is made available to him at the time and in the manner that *he* requires, he *will* adequately develop the skills to communicate, to cope with changing knowledge, and to interact with others in ways which enhance the welfare of all concerned.

It should be made clear that the question is not "Is the management or arrangement of learning conditions a desirable practice?" Clearly, the *arrangement* of conditions *is* necessary for effective learning. Rather, the question is "*How* are conditions to be arranged?" More specifically, "*Are conditions to be arranged for the purpose of helping the individual student learn and develop in personally satisfying ways, or are they to be arranged for the purpose of satisfying the needs of the instructor?*"

When school personnel arrange learning conditions or attempt to direct a student's thinking, learning and behaving in a manner that he finds personally unrewarding—irrevelant to his experiences and goals, they cannot expect anything but resistance on the part of the student. The student will demonstrate considerable ingenuity in devising the coping and surviving strategies he needs to avoid and escape what are for him contrived and meaningless learning activities. He will cut classes, feign illnesses, "underachieve," lie, daydream, cheat and openly resist. Nothing else can be expected when the student is legitimately concerned about his own needs and ambitions, and the school chooses to ignore or reject these concerns. Coercion and punishment *are* needed to have students perform in ways that are irrevelant to their goals, needs and values. Coercion is needed to manipulate students and to have them perform in ways to which they are generally opposed.

When students resist the teacher's efforts to have them comply with his demands, the teacher accuses the students of not being motivated to learn. The teacher fails to realize that the reason he finds it necessary to prod students is that the goals, content and processes of learning are in most cases inappropriate for the learning styles, capabilities and needs of the students. Evidence points to the fact that when the conditions and opportunities for learning are consonant with the student's predispositions to learn, the problem of motivating the student disappears. Accordingly the teacher's most fundamental responsibility is to make available a number of different kinds of opportunities and to provide the structure and assistance that each student needs to explore, discover and develop on his own terms.

ADULTS KNOW BEST

The second basic assumption that is implied in the unwarranted generalization about learning and development is that adults know best what is important, useful and of value to the young. The reasoning process goes something like the following: "The young do not know what is the true, the good and the beautiful. However, mature adults do. Consequently, the adults are obligated to present the true, the good and the beautiful to the young."

Many educators believe that the educational objectives of having students know the true, perform the good and value the beautiful can best be achieved by requiring students to complete a program in which the goals, content and processes of learning are quite carefully and clearly defined by educational "experts." They believe that when "experts" and "mature adults" devise a program of activities which circumscribe the specific truths and the particular skills and values to be acquired, the schools have provided the most essential conditions for all students to become constructive and responsible adults. Predictably under such an educational policy, the curriculum becomes comprised of facts, concepts and issues which the "experts" prize, but which *students* too often find irrevelant to their lives. Learning cycles become divorced from life cycles and from the reality the student knows. The student tends to perceive the content and process of schooling as having little relationship to his life.

When students are required to engage in learning activities which they do not find personally relevant, they require more time and have more difficulty mastering the involved tasks. Moreover, the purpose and meaning that students perceive in these activities are often different from those perceived by the teacher. Assuredly, students are learning in such situations, but they are not necessarily learning what the teacher wants them to learn. More likely they are learning that most classroom tasks and experiences are boring and meaningless, and are to be avoided whenever possible. When students are exposed to learning activities which they cannot relate to their own lives, the meaning which they acquire does not encourage further learning, rather it dissuades the learner from engaging in similar activities in the future. Teachers must accept the fact that meaningful learning is a highly personal process and it centers around the unique world of the learner. Consequently, if the goals, content and processes in schools are to be made relevant to the concerns, feelings and values of learners, the learners themselves will need to be given a significant role in determining the kinds of experiences which schools are to make available to them.

A SINGLE PROCESS

A third assumption found in the unwarranted generalization about human learning and development is that there is a single process which is appropriate for all learners. Many educators believe that it is desirable for all learners of a particular age to be guided through the same content at the same time in the same way. However, knowledge of individual differences indicates that no two learners respond to a given learning opportunity in the same way and for the same reasons at a particular point in time. Students differ in the rate of development of their physical, emotional and intellectual capabilities; in their experiences with age mates, parents and siblings; in their attitudes, values, concerns and ambitions; and in the ways all of these characteristics interact. The particular interacting characteristics of the individual student in turn result in the unique learning style that he brings to a learning situation.

We may infer from this that no single set of objectives, no single learning process, and no single period of time is appropriate for all learners to learn and develop optimally. No single method of grouping learners whether it be by age, sex, size, achievement test scores or I.Q. is capable of dealing with the significant learning predispositions which each student brings to a school task. To enable each learner to obtain the maximum benefit from his stay in school, and to provide the goals, content and processes of learning which are valid for each learner, the administration and the classroom teacher must tailor learning conditions and opportunities to each student's developmental style and unique profile of learning predispositions. Translated into everyday school practices, this means that concepts such as the regular classroom meeting, sequential learning and "adult-as-teacher" are not the most desirable procedures in all instances. In many cases independent study, self-selected groups, random learning and "student-as-teacher" are far more appropriate and effective approaches to learning.

It is tragic that with all of our advances in science and technology, the planning and providing of comparable advances in learning conditions is rarely found in the typical classroom. *We have the wherewithall to do what needs to be done, but the evidence is clear that most teachers are afraid or unwilling to give up old concepts and make the needed changes in our schools.* (13) It is dishonest, to say the least, that we convey to students that we believe in individualized learning conditions— in planning and providing conditions for each student to learn in terms of the abilities, level of motivation and problems that he brings to the school situation—and at the same time impose on him a common set of objectives, materials and procedures, and subject him to a system of evaluation which compares his capabilities to be successful with those of students who differ markedly.

A SINGLE CRITERION OF ACHIEVEMENT

Given the belief that all learners of a particular age should be guided through the same content at the same time and in the *same way,* it follows inexorably that the same criterion of achievement should apply to all children of that particular group. This belief is based on the assumption that a fixed standard of performance is equally applicable to all students in a group regardless of the individual differences in ability and motivation.

A clear illustration of this assumption in practice is the grade level concept. Most teachers are unwilling to give up the notion of grade level when establishing standards of academic performance. However, the different learning rates and styles of students indicates that the use of a single criterion of achievement is unwarranted and destructive in its effects on students. Within a given grade the range of abilities and learning rates often span several grades. For example, in an eighth grade class of 30 students the reading levels are likely to range from the fifth grade to the twelfth grade.

> Furthermore, a single child does not progress all of a piece: he tends to spurt ahead more rapidly in some areas than in others. Consequently, a difference of one grade between his reading attainment and his arithmetic attainment at the end of the second grade classification may be extended to a three- or four-grade difference by the end of his fifth year in school. . . . In brief . . . a fifth-grade teacher . . . is not a teacher of fifth-grade children. At a given time, he teaches third, fourth, fifth, sixth, seventh, eight and even ninth grades, as far as learner realities are concerned, even though all the pupils in his room may be labeled "fifth grade." (14, p. 3)

A grade level is a statistical concept and as such it describes only the average or midpoint in achievement of all of the students within the grade in question. The term grade level implies that approximately half of the group of students will perform at or above the midpoint and approximately half of the group will perform below the midpoint. Hence, when the school insists on grade level performance and above as the only acceptable levels of achievement for *all* students, it is arithmetically impossible for more than *half* of the students to pass. Consequently, a student who is viewed as a failure simply because he does not achieve at least the midpoint of the group is being dealt a serious injustice. Adherence to the statistical concept of grade level dooms a large percentage of learners to failure *before* they come to school. Students below grade level in ability and motivation would need to perform beyond their capabilities to succeed.

The case is the same with respect to a classroom evaluation method that stresses the midpoint and above of students' test scores as the only acceptable levels of achievement for *all* students. It is impossible for a student of less than average ability and motivation to receive a passing grade. Clearly, educational concepts such as grade level and classroom average are dishonest, destructive and totally unwarranted when attempting to identify and provide the most appropriate conditions for the individual student to learn and develop in personally and socially constructive ways.

EFFECTS ON THE SCHOOLING PROCESS

Closed Book

If it is believed that there is a best content, process and time for learning for all students, and that these are known, then it follows that the only ideas and beliefs that are of importance or value to a student in school and in his life are those preselected for him. That which is true and good is presented to students as a closed book. In a learning atmosphere such as this, students will not be given an opportunity to either present different ideas and hypotheses or to restate, redefine, or reassess their old ideas and values. Students will not be permitted to believe that what is known at this moment is only the most plausible hypothesis that can be formulated at this point in time, and they will not be given the chance to realize that what is true today may be fancy tomorrow and what is fancy today may be true tomorrow. If teachers believe that all of the truth is known and that which is of value has been predetermined, schooling becomes a tragic process of indoctrination and suppression of human potential.

Patent Truths

If in the mind of the teacher, the truth is known and values have been carefully and clearly defined, then it follows inexorably that there are right and wrong answers and solutions to questions and problems. Students are not to come to school to explore the different dimensions to questions or the varied solutions to problems, rather, they are to listen for, accept, and report back the right and best ways of doing things. Many students come to school with the assumption that their ideas, feelings and beliefs are of value, and that their views will be shown to have merit in the classroom. However, when these students enter the classroom they learn very quickly that no matter how plausible their ideas and hypotheses are to the resolution of issues, the teacher only rewards the "correct" answer.

Many teachers are quite impatient with and intolerant of a child who does not agree with the right answer. John Holt has told us much about the pervasiveness of these practices in his book *How Children Fail.* (19) One situation he describes deals with a student's wrong answer to an arithmetic problem. One day in class the students were reading their answers to the assigned arithmetic problems. All of the correct answers seemed to be flowing well until one student raised his hand to disagree with one of the reported answers. The teacher felt that the student's interruption was unnecessary, but decided finally to allow the student to speak. The boy said he didn't obtain the same answer as the other students did. He began to explain why he didn't when the teacher interrupted, not allowing him to complete his response. The teacher exclaimed that wrong answers are of no interest or value to anyone. As might be predicted, the boy did not voice his opinion again on any other issue in class.

Other kinds and effects of intolerance to students' different ideas and ways of performing have been described by Jonathan Kozol in *Death at an Early Age*. (25) Kozol describes how an art teacher had a preconceived notion of good drawings and had selected such drawings from the work of her former students and displayed them in her class. One day the teacher approached one of her students in class, and, after a perfunctory examination of his drawings, tore them up and labeled them garbage because they did not compare favorably with the drawings illustrated in front of the class. Not only was the teacher's judgment of the student's work unfair, but her action had a corrosive effect on the student's perception of himself as a competent and capable person. How humiliating it must have been to the student to have the teacher, in front of the entire class, tear his drawings into strips and deposit them in the wastebasket as garbage. Many teachers are unaware that their intolerance of any ideas or performances not in accord with those that they value may destroy a child's creative potential and his feelings of self-worth.

Prevention of Inquiry

If all of the truth is known, and all questions have right answers, it follows that students will learn only when they listen to all of the wisdom that the teachers possess. Many teachers believe this and conduct their classes accordingly. In most classrooms the behavior that is sought and rewarded is passive listening and acceptance of the ideas and values of the teacher. The classroom is structured in such a way that the role of the teacher and the role of the students are quite carefully and clearly defined. A primary rule of the game is to refrain from asking questions unless they are for clarification of the known. Students are not encouraged to inquire about and find meaning in the reality which they know. Often, in fact, the learner is made aware that if he asks questions or expresses his views honestly he runs the risk of physical punishment, failure and perhaps expulsion.

Many teachers are unable or unwilling to accept the fact that the student ultimately must find out for himself what is true, good and beautiful. They do not understand that the particular concept, principle or answer itself is unimportant in relation to *how* and *why* we reach a particular conclusion. Many teachers fail to realize that meaningful learning is a continual process of personal discovery, that the individual student must (a) state his doubts, questions, feelings and values, (b) identify and discuss all possible implications of his views and proposed behaviors for himself and others, (c) identify the most plausible hypotheses and approaches to solutions and (d) implement what seems to be the most effective, valid or moral alternative. While there is agreement that when students have completed their education they should be resourceful and creative enough to identify accurately and resolve satisfactorily the many kinds of problems they will face as individuals in a society, the nature of the school process in most instances does not allow for the development of the necessary skills. Provisions for honest, free and thorough inquiry and discourse—the only adequate avenue for becoming resourceful and creative individuals who are constructive and responsible in facing the reality of self and society—are conspicuously absent from the agenda of most classroom teachers.

Compliance

The basic purpose of controlled learning, which is clear to both the teacher and the student, is compliance. This term, however, is rarely used in the schools; instead we are told that children need to be taught cooperative behavior, how to be good citizens and how to act as mature persons. The demand to comply is made not only of young children but also of high school and college students. For example, Friedenberg (8, p. 185) points out that in the typical high school "students learn for four years that they cannot so much as walk down the hall to the library or toilet without written permission." This is, as Hart points out, a disadvantageous schooling process.

> The six-foot tall, 180-pound senior who must prove his right to relieve himself or consult a reference work, even if he has no class at the moment, may a few months later be operating a $100,000 machine in a factory, driving a huge truck, or wandering a college campus wholly on his own. (17, p. 7–8)

Regardless of the arguments and logic that administrators give for school rules and policies, it is obvious that what they want from students is compliance to predetermined notions of what is true and good. The child comes to school curious, excited and eager to explore and discover, yet these learning predispositions do not show themselves for very long. The school's procedures, in a calculated and systematic fashion, chip away the child's capabilities to think, feel and respond as an independent person.

Coercion and Punishment

If the teacher feels that his obligation in the classroom is to have students comply with what he believes to be of value, then the teacher undoubtedly will employ coercive and perhaps punitive techniques when students are reluctant to accommodate him. As Holt (19) points out, coercive and punitive techniques can be employed openly and directly in the form of ridicule, sarcasm or physical punishment, or they can be expressed in very subtle and indirect ways by the withholding of approval and recognition and by the withdrawal of affection and attention. He describes how teachers use a variety of subtle techniques to make students afraid or ashamed enough to submit to their demands. Teachers, with a single gesture or word, remind students that retribution is in store for those who are reluctant to conform. Whatever the technique, students tend to feel that survival in the classroom is predicated on earning the acceptance and approval of the teacher, and to receive these, students must play the game according to the teacher's rules. The basic weapon of the schools is fear, a weapon often treacherously wielded.

A very basic educational, if not moral issue that schools must face when they have students learn through coercion, fear and punishment, is whether or not what is learned is in any way constructive or useful to the learner or society. When students are *told* what to think, say and do each minute they are in school, and when they must comply with the teachers' demands to avoid punishment, can we say that these students are learning in a way which will enhance the development of a *democratic* society? Can we even say that these students are learning in any sense connected with *education?* (17)

Coping Strategies

Once students have received the message that punitive techniques will be employed to have them conform or accommodate the teacher, they will devise whatever strategies they believe are needed to cope with or survive their stay in the classroom. When it comes to staying out of trouble or obtaining satisfactory grades, figuring out the teacher is without question the greatest single demand made on students. Students seek clues from the teacher to help them cope with the stresses in the classroom. They search the teacher's facial expression, tone or posture to find out how to behave and what the right answers are.

Obviously, some students are not skilled in reading the teacher. Other students can read the teacher, but are unable to develop the necessary coping strategies. Still other students are unwilling to play the game at all; they refuse to meet the unfair demands of the teacher, and they refuse to be subjected to coercive and punitive techniques in the classroom. Predictably, rebellion and withdrawal are exhibited by many students in an effort to reduce or totally eliminate school pressures.

Destruction of Individuality

The most serious, as well as the most common, consequence of controlled learning and its practices of requiring students to falsify their behaviors is the destruction of a student's freedom to think, feel and value in an open and sincere fashion. When the student submits to coercion and threat he foregoes the right to be a free and authentic participant in the reality that he knows.

> He loses his power to make use of all those capacities which make him truly human: his reason ceases to operate; he may be intelligent, he may be capable of manipulating things and himself, but he accepts as truth that which those who have power over him call the truth. He loses his power of love, for his emotions are tied (in a symbiotic relationship) to those who he depends. He loses his moral sense, for his inability to question and criticize those in power stultifies his moral judgment with regard to anybody and anything . . . Indeed, freedom is the necessary condition to happiness as well as of virtue; freedom, not in the sense of the ability to make arbitrary choices and not freedom from necessity, but freedom to realize that which one potentially is, to fulfill the true nature of man according to the laws of his existence. (10, pp. 247–248)

The belief that a predetermined set of learning conditions must be imposed on students is unwarranted. Yet this unwarranted belief constitutes a basic premise on which are based many school policies and practices which always restrict, and often destroy, a student's chance to engage in logical and creative thinking, to feel and behave as a free agent, and to see himself as having worth as a person.

3

THE PURSUIT

For many students schools provide a curriculum that is a distortion of the reality they see and know on television and in the streets. Students are often required to read materials and engage in processes that are totally divorced from their concerns, experiences and learning styles. In short, what students all too often encounter in school is a protracted stay in an environment that bears slight resemblance to the reality that they find outside the school.

The problem of irrelevant school experiences has many dimensions; but for our purposes we will consider five examples. First, much of the content taught in the classroom is not in keeping with the reality the learner knows. Second, the learner's reality is often regarded as immaterial in the classroom. Third, much of the content that teachers emphasize and consider important is trivia. Fourth, what is pertinent to a subject is often not shown to be relevant to the learner. Fifth, the processes of learning in which students are required to participate are often not appropriate to either the students' needs or to the performance capabilities they are expected to demonstrate as adults.

DISTORTIONS OF REALITY

Students at virtually every level of education frequently are required to read materials which portray life as though few people have problems and that those who do can immediately find satisfactory solutions. For

20

OF IRRELEVANCE

example, elementary school readers almost invariably present to children the picture that family members always live together, that all people have adequate food, clothing and shelter, and that virtually no hatred, prejudice or violence exists in the world. Although there are some efforts to use "realistic" reading materials in the schools, the overwhelming majority of our elementary school readers describe a storybook world in which there are only happy children, happy parents, happy pets and happy neighbors. Rarely do these readers include stories or situations in which children are sick, handicapped or perplexed by personal problems. Other texts talk about how freedom and justice are found only in America, with opportunities for economic and social advancement open to anyone regardless of religion, race, national origin or sex. Yet many youngsters who read these books experience discrimination and poverty and live in dilapidated buildings that are infested with rats and roaches. They may have no more than one set of clothing, no bathtub, and no father. How dishonest the school must appear to such children.

These reading books rarely talk about the poor, the unfortunate or the disadvantaged. How many children, or for that matter college graduates, know that Indians, whose average life expectancy is less than 25 years because of poverty, disease and despair, exist on certain American reservations? Are reading materials which fail to portray accurately the real world adequately preparing youths to become concerned and responsible citizens capable of handling the complex economic, political and social problems present in our society?

FAILURE TO VALUE LEARNER'S WORLD

Not only do some schools inaccurately portray the real world to students, but they also systematically avoid providing opportunities for students to interpret the experiences they are having outside the classroom. Rare is the school where students can report their personal observations, express their ideas, engage in discussion and debate, and interpret and evaluate the meaning of their life outside the classroom. Many schools deny or discount the reality that the student sees and knows. They often minimize the significance that events have in the life of a student. In so doing, the schools are training our youth to be disadvantaged—unconcerned about and ill-equipped to deal with the entire range of human problems that go unresolved day after day.

Are these the goals of education? If not, one wonders how schools expect children to develop the understanding and skills they need to deal adequately with the problems (including poverty, alienation, despair, drug abuse, suicide and war) that confront them *now* when the existence and/or importance of such problems are systematically placed out of the context of the school. Often it is argued that there is no need to bring these problems into the school because the child will learn in due course about the problems which face adults. Some of these very same people are the first to say that "students aren't aware of what is really going on" or "they don't have enough understanding of the issues to offer any intelligent solution to problems." We deny the existence or importance of problems to students, and then we blame them for not understanding the issues. How dishonest the schools are and what a great disservice they render in depriving students of so much knowledge at an early age and in denying them so many of the skills that they will need to perform as competent adults.

If we truly believe that education *must* be different for each student to have him learn in reasonably satisfying ways, then the school must face up to the fact that it has as one of its major responsibilities helping the individual student make some sense out of the world in which he now finds himself. The school must begin where the learner is in order to have him go *beyond* his present performance capabilities. Consequently, one might well ask if a detailed analysis of *The Scarlet Letter* and *Silas Marner* will help prepare students to deal with the personal problems and the issues that concern them, or if memorizing the names of the Roman emperors and wars will equip youths with the skills they need to grapple competently with the perplexing political and social problems they face. This should not be interpreted as meaning that the entire curriculum should be comprised of personal and social issues and problems, or that classrooms should be used for the purpose of providing group psychotherapy. However, if we want the learner to move toward attaining the highest levels of personal and social development that are within his capabilities—to move toward *what could be*—we must begin with *what is*.

TRIVIA

It seems incongruous that a society such as ours, which has developed such advanced technological capabilities, is faced with such alarming incidences of alcoholism, drug abuse, crime and mental disorders. In light of these crisis situations in the area of human relations, it is difficult to believe that the typical school curriculum places very little emphasis on the antecedents and consequences of man's negative and destructive attitudes, feelings and behavior tendencies. Instead, far too many schools ask students to memorize the precise date on which a particular event took place. This is required of a student who is searching for answers to the complexities that exist in *his* world. If the school is indeed to teach him to "understand the world in which he lives," it will have to deal with *his* questions.

> Why do I live in the slums? Why do people fight so much? Why aren't there any Negroes living on our block? Why do I get so angry when someone takes something that belongs to me? Why do we have to hide certain parts of our body? These and many other questions that may perplex the child usually go unanswered in school. (6, p. 131)

To be sure some factual information is needed to acquire concepts, to reason and to solve problems. But it is a disturbing inconsistency to demand that students memorize isolated facts and study that which is quite remote from their lives when communication media are making us increasingly aware of the many serious and complex problems that face us each day. In no period of history has man exhibited such paradoxical behavior. Although we are surrounded by problems which should be of the utmost concern, their existence and importance is almost always submerged when we look at the process of education.

What is equally sad is that much of the information students are asked to memorize is catalogued and placed in reference works. Are not all the U. S. presidents listed in correct order in a number of places that are easily accessible? Are not the leading export products of each South American country also listed in reference works? Why then does the child need to memorize them? Will instant recall of such information aid him in solving the problems he will face as an adult? How many adults can recall the names of all of the presidents in correct order? If trivia is of little importance to adults can it mean anything to children? Adults and children are concerned primarily with their own behavior and its relationship to the environment in which they live. However, much of what man considers to be precious and of real value in life cannot be placed in reference works and is rarely emphasized in schools. What reference work articulates to the child how he is to adapt to a changing environment or to solve the problems of drug abuse, pollution prejudice, mental illness, and war?

FAILURE TO DEMONSTRATE RELEVANCE

Teachers somehow assume that if they see the relevance in what they are presenting to students, the students also see the importance and wisdom involved. However, this is not the case. Since the backgrounds, life styles, concerns and goals of students are almost invariably different from those of the teacher, certain activities may be perceived by students as having relevance, while many tasks and materials appear to them as having no relationship to their lives. Moreover, the classroom teacher often does little to change this state of affairs.

The inclusion of current issues and problems in the curriculum does not in itself make the learning process relevant to students. Teachers often discuss current issues and problems either from a purely historical outlook, with little consideration of future implications for students, or on a level of abstraction that is remote from what students have experienced.

What a student freely chooses to learn is that which he believes is of value to him and relevant to his life. If the student fails to see the personal relevance of particular activities, learning may still take place out of fear of academic failure or punishment. However, since the effect of such fears is avoidance behavior, there is little likelihood that the knowledge and skills mastered under adverse conditions will be retained by students for any significant period of time. If the student believes that he can in no way relate the performance requirements in the class-room to his own needs in life, temporarily acquired performance capa-bilities quite likely will be discarded at the student's earliest convenience.

IRRELEVANT PROCESSES

Up to this point we have been discussing irrelevance largely in terms of the content, subject matter or materials students encounter in the classroom. Irrelevance, of course, occurs with respect to the process of learning and teaching. With few exceptions, the routines in which students participate require only the skills of memory. When problem-solving, discovery or inquiry processes are employed, they too often deal with *trivia*. It is hard to believe that teachers would have students utilize discovery approaches to track down a fact that is insignificant; yet many teachers do it. Imagine a teacher requiring students to discover the number of plumes that Cyrano de Bergerac had in his hat. When students are forced to search for an unimportant message, they are probably learning only how ingenious the teacher can be at devising meaningless experiences.

No one can quarrel with the desirability of having students explore and discover the world in which they live; but, to be sure, man was not given the potential of developing highly advanced thinking to be used on trivia. There are critically important issues facing man that need immediate attention, and it is these issues which should engage man's imagination and his greatest wisdom and skills.

SUMMARY

If teachers would ask themselves whether they would study materials or practice at tasks which they could not relate to their own lives, the response undoubtedly would be a resounding *no!* Few teachers would willingly set aside periods of time each day to sit at a desk and work religiously at transforming fractions, diagraming sentences or memorizing the names of the known elements in chemistry as ends in themselves. They would find these daily exercises personally meaningless and would consider the time set aside for these tasks wasted. Yet these are precisely the kinds of experiences that many teachers require of their students both inside and outside the classroom. Moreover, most of the student's out-of-school experiences and problems are avoided or denied by the school. In so doing, the school fails to convey to the student the value it has to offer him. In time, many students see the school's rejection of their reality as a rejection of themselves.

The school's distortions of reality and its rejection of the reality the learner knows can do nothing but harm to students. When life inside the classroom fails to relate to life outside the classroom, apathy, boredom, resentment, alienation, disruptive behavior and physical violence are quite predictable of students, especially those who suffer substantial frustration outside the school. Even the students who are academically successful fail to learn in many ways that are constructive to themselves and society. They may even be learning that the problems people face are to be ignored and that involvement in the resolution of social problems is best avoided.

There is a tragic irony in requiring students to study materials and engage in processes which they find irrelevant to life. The very institutions which should prepare youths to become effective problem solvers and concerned citizens are snuffing out the candle of critical thinking and contributing substantially to the development of social incompetence. This is especially true with respect to those students who have been unable to rise from the bottom of our social system. While all students have been victimized to some degree by schools' emphasis on the memorization of large quantities of facts, rather than on complex problem-solving skills, the socially disadvantaged have been especially hurt. They do not have the resources to compensate for an irrelevant education, although others often have home and social group experiences which help them salvage something from a weak education. While the schools, with all of their innovations and technological hardware, have failed the disadvantaged and advantaged alike, their failure to provide some means for the disadvantaged to cope with life and to become fully functioning persons has been especially tragic.

The implications of the relevant experience hypothesis for planning classroom learning opportunities are evident. One of the schools' and teachers' major tasks is to provide materials and activities in which students can find personal meaning and which are applicable to their lives outside the classroom. To handle this task adequately the teacher needs to ask himself how the subject matter he is teaching and the facilities which are at his disposal can be brought to bear on the important issues that his students face. He needs to provide opportunities for students to play the major role, both in identifying the important issues of the day and in searching for their solutions.

Schools must openly and honestly face up to what is reality for the students; schools can no longer deny students the opportunity to raise and examine the issues and problems of our time. If each student is denied the opportunity to develop adequately the skills for sensitively dealing with the vital issues and complex problems of the twentieth century, the schools must be prepared to accept the blame when students fail to learn and develop in socially constructive ways. If the schools themselves demonstrate little concern for the problems which deeply affect the rights and welfare of all, they cannot expect the students to be motivated. The students have not failed! They have learned their lessons well: conform, perform feats of memory, and value the irrelevant and trivial over people and their problems!

4

DESTRUCTIVE

To be sure, the individual teacher who employs strategies of coercion and control, and who utilizes irrelevant content and processes is to be held accountable for most of the students' failure to learn in personally and socially advantageous ways. However, there are often other school forces at work helping students to fail. There are many policies which administrators establish and which teachers and administrators collectively promote, which pervade each classroom and have a corrosive influence on students' efforts to learn. These policies constitute what might be termed *institutional processes*. It is some of the more pernicious institutional processes that we will examine in this chapter.

COMPETITION

Coming in first is a basic goal of U.S. economic and political philosophy. This emphasis in our culture has a profound effect on the schooling process and on its participants. Extraordinary demands are placed on all schools to turn out a product which is superior to products of previous years. The message the school receives is in turn quickly and clearly communicated to the student: *The superior and most competent per-*

INSTITUTIONAL PROCESSES

formers are the most highly sought and rewarded. The highest paying jobs and the most prestigeous colleges and graduate schools are open only to the top students. To earn the status of being good, each school engages in a twofold process: it continually raises the minimum acceptable levels of academic achievement for *all* students, and it establishes policies to distinguish the superior students from the less talented. Both of these policies exert extraordinary pressures on students to perform at increasingly higher levels. The schools are demanding that all students jump to whatever levels the bar is raised. When students manage to perform at the highest level that has been set, the schools interpret this to mean that greater demands should be placed on students. Schools are unwilling to draw the line and say, "Enough," even though their demands outstrip both their ability to provide appropriate instruction and their ability to arrange reasonably satisfying consequences for students.

Effects on Students

Emphasis on Memorization. One effect of intense competition in education is that many students are required to perform difficult feats of memory or to study highly advanced materials. For some students, these materials are irrelevant to their outlooks, experiences and goals. When competition characterizes the schooling process, the *individual* student's needs and unique talents are necessarily placed outside the context of education.

Mental Health.   The effects of competition are disadvantageous also with respect to many students' mental health. For example, the Gordons, in their book, *The Blight on the Ivy,* report substantial shifts in the *primary* reasons why adolescents and young adults (aged 13–24) seek psychiatric help. They found that:

> stresses related to education drove nearly three-fourths of the youthful patients to psychiatrists' offices in the 1960's as compared to only one-third in the early 1950's. Certainly, other problems are upsetting today's youth—worries about jobs, about military service, about nuclear war. But the majority of teenagers and young adults who sought psychiatric help blame their troubles on the strain of getting an education. (15, p. 12)

Cheating.   Cheating is another consequence of academic competition. Many students believe that cheating is the only alternative they have for coping with excessive academic pressures. Evidence indicates that cheating occurs more frequently among students who feel that teachers are making unrealistic demands on them. (49) Our most able performers maintain that the importance of winning justifies the use of illegitimate means to succeed in school.

The Dropout.   An obvious consequence of competition, and one of the more tragic, is the dropout. A basic generalization from psychological research which applies is that a person can experience only so much failure and then he may be expected to engage in withdrawal or avoidance behaviors. Hoping to avoid future unsuccessful experiences, several hundreds of thousands of school age individuals leave the classroom each year before they have completed their twelve years of basic education. The most common causes of attrition are not marriage, pregnancy and military service but "poor performance in school subjects," "lack of interest in school subjects," and "unsatisfying student-teacher relationships," (20) all of which are brought about in no small part by pressures to meet unrealistic standards. Many schools are unaware or unconcerned that when they continually raise performance standards (without improving the quality of instruction) and apply a single set of performance criteria to all students, the number of students who are academically and psychologically suited for school becomes fewer and fewer.

Perhaps the two most disadvantageous consequences of competition in the schools are that the act of learning itself becomes degraded and positive human relationships become threatened or destroyed.

The Corruption of Learning.   It is currently accepted by many youths that we go to school not to explore, discover and find meaning in the wonderful reality which man has before him, but to get out of school what is needed to win or be a success in the marketplace. Winning requires that students take the right courses and secure the right grades and symbols of achievement. Education has become a game wherein success is not to be achieved by an authentic interaction of people's concerns, ideas and values, but by identifying the rules of the schooling process very early and following them religiously. How we have corrupted learning and the young! Before our youths are out of childhood they have become more concerned about the skills they need for success in the marketplace than about exploring, discovering and developing the best that is in them.

The Destruction of Personal Relationships.   The concerns for academic survival and status have required students to develop the most practical strategies they can to come out ahead.

> Both the classroom and the playing field are places where you try to make it and learn the techniques for making it that alienate you least from your peers. The overall rules are the same in both: learn the ropes; don't get hung up; always be friendly, sincere and creative. And win! (9, p. 14)

However, winning without alienating oneself to some degree from others is almost impossible. In many instances the schooling experience is seen by students as a war. Each day they feel they must try to defeat each other for prizes, grades and scholarships. When a student wins, he is resented by those whom he has defeated; when he loses he is often hostile toward those who have defeated him. Clearly, no single process is more destructive of friendships and positive interpersonal relationships during childhood and adolescence than the school's unrelenting emphasis on winning.

Is Competition Necessary?

Most educators argue that competition in school is desirable, even necessary if a young person is to be adequately prepared to find and keep a reasonably satisfying job in the marketplace. However, such an assumption is false. People enter occupations usually when there is a chance of success; they generally avoid jobs they believe will surely result in failure or dissatisfaction. This point suggests that competition in school is permissable when each student has at least a moderate chance of being successful. The use of competition is indefensible when the outcome of a competitive situation is a foregone conclusion. For example, competition is dishonest and destructive when the achievement level or test score of a 90 I.Q. student is to be compared to the achievement level or test score of an 130 I.Q. student. But, while the condition of "a moderate chance of success" is a necessary one, it alone is not sufficient to warrant the use of competition in school.

Although the probability of success may be moderate or high for a student, he may not have the personality dispositions or values which make him able and willing to engage in performance rivalries. I would hasten to add that if one of our educational goals *is* to help the student acquire the skills to compete in situations where there is little chance of success, then the schools need to provide the conditions in which students—*all* of them—learn to cope satisfactorily with this kind of competition. The conditions needed to acquire these skills, however, should not be confused with the conditions students need to acquire the skills to communicate effectively, reason logically, cope with changing knowledge and deal competently with the personal and social problems they encounter each day. The basic issue, of course, is that competition is not a necessary condition for successful school learning.

For too long teachers and administrators have been deceiving themselves and the public by insisting that students need to compete to be motivated to learn. These school personnel have failed to make the distinction between motivating a student to complete tasks and achieve goals appropriate for him, and motivating a student to succeed in relation to other students. Students learn in far more satisfying ways when materials, goals and rewards are individualized for them than when they are exposed to a common course of study and are required to compete for passing grades. We know enough about human behavior to say unequivocally that when we provide *individualized conditions* for each student to learn, e.g., appropriate kinds of programmed learning, discovery learning, contingency contracting and vertically continuous materials and tasks, competition becomes totally irrelevant to the issues of motivation and learning.

Competition and Equality of Opportunity

In recent years there has been considerable concern about the civil rights of each individual, both inside and outside the area of education. One consequence of this concern has been to place considerable emphasis on the concept of equality of opportunity. However, when we talk about equality of opportunity, we need to distinguish between equal conditions to learn and develop and equal right and access to whatever conditions one needs to learn and develop. When we fail to make this distinction, and when we view equality of opportunity as referring to equal conditions, then equality of opportunity becomes a deceptive and destructive concept. In our competitive social system, equality of opportunity is not given to mean that each individual is to be provided with the most appropriate conditions for actualizing his potentialities. It means, instead, that each individual is to be given the same conditions to succeed within the existing goals and values of our society; and this means ultimately that the most suited can become the most successful, and the least suited are given little chance to rise from the bottom. When conditions for learning are made to fit into our basic social philosophy of competition, equality of opportunity bears little, if any, resemblance to appropriateness of opportunity. We cannot establish learning conditions and achievement standards for all students without regard to their different capabilities, concerns and experiences. If students of different predispositions compete in a setting where the goals, materials and processes are the same for all students, there will be only the success of the suited, and the whole issue of meaningful and relevant human learning and development for each student becomes a tragic farce. What each student needs is appropriate or adequate conditions, not equal conditions, and to have these, the concept of *equality of opportunity* must be given to mean equal right and access to whatever conditions are needed to learn and develop.

ADMINISTRATIVE DESIGN

Destructive effects on learning are not only produced by teachers' behavior, but also by an irrelevant curriculum and competition. The kinds of policies and practices that administrators establish may also have a corrosive influence on the kind of learning and teaching that takes place in the classroom. Two of the most disadvantageous influences that the adminstrator exerts on learning deal with his preoccupation with efficiency and his belief that the responsibility for educational administration resides only with him.

Concern for Efficiency

The primary concern of most administrators is to establish policies which provide for an economical and smoothly functioning school. Many administrators view the operation of schools in a manner similar to the operation of industries. An analogy between schools and industries was made in the October 1958 issue of *Fortune*. The author maintained that "the schools, no less than the automobile industry, have an inescapable production problem." For him the most fundamental task of the school is not much different from the basic task of General Motors. The school's job, he maintained, is to "optimize the number of students and to minimize the input of man-hours and capital." It is overwhelmingly clear that schools and classrooms, like GM, are organized for the purpose of turning out a uniform or homogeneous product. Unlike GM, however, the production failures of the school are blamed on the product, rather than on the process.

To summarize, our public schools are organized to facilitate administration rather than learning; and administrative efficiency is of such importance in most schools that it compromises and perhaps destroys students' freedom to learn and teachers' freedom to facilitate learning. (47)

Scapegoating the Community.   To be sure, the people in each community often attempt to impose their political and religious beliefs on the school board, the principal and the teachers. However, administrators err seriously when they scapegoat the community for the schools' indefensible policies and practices. Administrators can blame the community for insufficient funds, but they cannot blame the community for the school's pernicious policies and practices; they cannot hide behind a statement such as "I am working within the framework of what the community wants." Assuredly some communities do not want the schools to provide formal instruction on specific topics, e.g., "sexual development and behavior." However, *communities do not pressure schools to establish general policies and practices which prevent constructive learning and teaching from taking place.* The charge of providing the conditions for learning has been given to the school; and it is quite clear that notions of what constitutes success and failure and what is the nature of constructive learning and teaching are formed by and within the school; they are not dictated by the community.

Consequences to Students.   When operational efficiency and the needs of administrators are valued over the needs of students, highly arbitrary and at times destructive practices are employed in the classroom. Under such circumstances the content and process of schooling may be totally incompatible with students' needs. There may be little honest concern for individual differences in learning rate and style. There may be no concern over the effects of school policies and practices on a student's self-concept. Consequently, the student comes to believe that his failure or success hangs on his ability to play the game and on chance. He begins to believe to a large degree that he is not valued as an individual with unique talents and needs, and in time, he comes to feel that he doesn't really count as a person.

Meaning of Educational Administration

Many administrators believe there is no need for close communication with a teacher unless he and his class present serious problems to the school's operation. As a consequence, a great many teachers fail to receive quality supervision of their actual classroom behaviors. The administrators' lack of close communication with teachers invites the criticism that administrators show little concern for teachers' plights in the classroom. Consequently, when they do confer, many teachers are often reluctant to consider an administrator's suggestions for improving their teaching situations.

Other administrators, however, take a very different point of view concerning their role. They deal with teachers in the same way they expect teachers to deal with students. They believe that their job is to shape the behaviors of their teachers along the lines of their own personal conceptions of good teaching. They over-supervise teachers in the hope of eliciting compliance. The impact of over-supervision on teachers has been documented by Minuchin and others. (32) For example, at one school they found that "the principal approved of teachers who could hold the children by a 'personal magnetism' and keep up with the sophisticated urban culture of the parent body." At a second school . . .

> the principal valued the competence of his teachers in keeping good control under all circumstances. The teachers echoed the principal's stress on good deportment, manners, self-control, and cleanliness as goals held up to the children. Translated for adults, as decorum and compliance, they became a paradigm of behavior for everybody in the school. (32, p. 65)

The administrators who over-supervise or encourage compliance believe either that teachers need to be controlled or that they prefer to be led, or both. Many administrators believe that teachers will work toward the achievement of an educational goal *only* if the proper kinds of behavioral controls are applied. (44) Many administrators have absolutely no conception of the nature of the democratic process. They may invite counsel, and they may state that every faculty member has a right to express his opinion; but when it comes to decision-making, there is no sharing of power or responsibility. More often than not administrators *tell* the faculty what has been decided. They view democracy as benevolent dictatorship.

Many, perhaps most, administrators fail to realize that their basic responsibility is to organize materials and equipment, and arrange conditions in such a way that both teachers and students are able to work together in identifying and achieving their own educational goals. The administrator is not to decide the goals and roles of other people. *All of the people directly affected by a decision must have a share of the power and responsibility in the decision-making process.*

PROPHECY, PREJUDICE AND SCAPEGOATING

Prophecy. When the schools place inordinate emphasis on efficiency, promote a philosophy of competitiveness, and employ a single set of learning and achievement criteria for nearly all students, a highly effective system for predicting academic failures and successes becomes established very early in the schooling process. (7) What seems to happen in many cases is that an ability level with regard to each child's competencies is established when the child first comes to school. This established ability level then becomes the teacher's guide as to the performances he can expect to observe in the child. This expectation is often passed on from grade to grade, and the school views and treats the child in a way that encourages the development and continuance of the expected response patterns. For example, many children are labeled early as slow or low in abilities needed to be successful with particular tasks. They tend to be viewed and treated in subsequent grades as inadequate individuals, and this encourages the continuance of disadvantageous response patterns. In short, teachers tend to determine very early in the child's education whether or not he will be successful, and they come to expect and encourage the child to perform only in terms of the predicted ways. The tragic consequence of teachers' expectations is that few students are given an opportunity to disappoint their teachers. Moreover, many students are viewed in an unfavorable way when they show improvement that is not predicted by the teacher. This is noted, for example, by the Rosenthal and Jacobson research on slow-track children.

> When these "slow-track" children were in the control group, where little intellectual gain was expected of them, they were rated more unfavorably by their teachers if they did show gains in I.Q. The more they gained, the more unfavorably they were rated. Even when the slow track children were in the experimental group, where greater intellectual gains were expected of them, they were not rated as favorably with respect to their control-group peers as were the children of

the high track and the medium track. Evidently it is likely to be difficult for a slow-track child, even if his I.Q. is rising, to be seen by his teacher as well adjusted and as a potentially successful student. (45, p. 22)

When a single course of study and a single criterion of achievement are applied to all students, and if the teacher behaves toward some students as though they are competent and toward other students as though they are incompetent, he runs a very good chance of producing in his students the very behaviors he expects of them. Moreover, a teacher is not likely to change his beliefs and expectations about students, even in the face of evidence which clearly dictates a change.

Prejudice. In many instances students are sorted, and expectations about their performances are established largely on the basis of their skin color. However, the setting of expectations on the basis of color is no ordinary sorting procedure. It is often accompanied by the most destructive school conditions and practices to be found anywhere.

Herbert Kohl (24) and Jonathon Kozol (25) have seen at first hand and have described in detail the appalling conditions that are to be found in slum schools, especially black ghetto schools. They report that many teachers in these schools are grossly incompetent and in many cases emotionally disturbed. The students may have substitute teachers for several years at a stretch. In many ghetto classrooms perceptions of the physical environment are dominated by cracked walls, peeling paint, bare light bulbs, broken windows and the smell of urine. The irony is that the American flag and a picture of Abraham Lincoln are also found in the same classrooms.

Kozol states quite emphatically that there are no conditions more effective for producing failure and for breeding hatred and violence than the prejudice, ridicule, sarcasm and treachery that are found in so many black ghetto schools. In many instances black students are punished for no reason except for their failure to show "respect" to teachers who behind the students' backs call them "niggers." The abusive teachers believe that the punishment "socializes" the students and "teaches them a lesson." The lesson they learn, however, is not what the teacher intended; as Kozol points out, the students learn that violence is the proper measure to take when other procedures fail.

We do not need revolutionary or militant groups to preach hate to children in ghettos to have these children hate us; the schools do it for them. The psychological and physical treachery that exists in many schools, especially in black ghetto schools, produces in many children only a desire for revenge. It may take the form of violence on a teacher, school or city. The following rhyme perhaps summarizes the destructive effects that black ghetto schools have on many youths.

> They said they knew my kind and they checked off my name
> As primitive and unsuited to succeed in the schooling game.
> But succeed I did; I learned my lesson well.
> I learned to hate, as riots in the cities tell.

It is most unfortunate that so much expensive research is being conducted to establish what is obvious to anyone who wants to see the conditions that exist in slum communities and schools. We don't need developmental psychologists to tell us about the restricted vocabulary and retarded language patterns of slum children. We don't need urban sociologists to tell us about the lack of father models, the devastating effects of poverty, and the sense of hopelessness that is pervasive in slum communities. We do not need educational psychologists to research carefully childrens' response styles in slum schools. Instead, we need to commit our money, our resources and ourselves to major educational and social reform.

Scapegoating.   When students fail or receive low grades, many schools maintain that failure occurs because students are not of the quality to measure up to necessary standards. The argument goes something like the following: "Many students from a particular home or social background are not ready either intellectually, motivationally or socially to perform at the minimum acceptable levels within the classroom." Granted, this is true if a single set of performance standards is applied to all students regardless of their differences in ability and motivation. However, as was discussed in Chapter 2, a single course of study and a single set of achievement criteria for all students is undesirable.

Many schools maintain that they are not failures because they cannot alter what children experience at home. They claim that the social backgrounds of students are overwhelming and decisive in school learning, and that for children who are socially disadvantaged, schools can exert very little influence on their behaviors. These statements are indefensible. Although there is evidence to support the assumption that during the first few years of life a child's home background is of particular importance in the development of intelligence and learning patterns, there is also evidence which indicates that the schools may have a considerable influence on the lives of children. From their study and comparison of several schools, Minuchin and others conclude that *"the schools affected the lives and functioning of the children in ways that were pervasive and perhaps profound."* (32, p. 390) They also found that

... under some conditions, the uniqueness and power of schooling is such that its impact may be strong even in areas that are usually shaped by the home and even if home and school orientation are not congruent. (32, p. 392)

It is sad indeed that educators believe that the *school* is to be applauded when the student is successful, but the *student* is to blame when he is unsuccessful. The process is to receive credit for the successes without being held accountable for the failures. The school is the only system in which the product is held accountable for the shortcomings and faulty operations of the process. The school sorts students and expects and encourages them to perform in certain ways, rarely giving them a chance to do otherwise, and then does not want to be held accountable for its effects. The time has come when we must call a spade a spade. *It is the process and not the product which must be held accountble.*

It is often assumed that the teacher's classroom practices are closely supervised by administrators and that he has little freedom in his classroom. However, close supervision is rarely in evidence. "Today, a school is usually a collection of rooms in which individual teachers conduct their classes just about as they please." (17, p. 72) It may be inferred that teachers as a group are responsible for most of the school's failure to start with each student where he is, to demonstrate the relevance of different subject areas to students' lives, to involve students in group decision-making processes and to establish appropriate criteria of achievement for each student.

We cannot blame the family or social background of the student, nor can we blame the student himself because he has low intelligence or is not motivated. These are scapegoats to draw attention away from the school and its personnel as the responsible agents for facilitating educational success.

> The obligation is not in the people who are different, but is rather in the professional, to learn to deal with a wide variety of students. If a physician's patient is not successfully treated with penicillin, he moves to sulpha or to another form of treatment. The medical model is that the obligation is the physician's to do something about the problem . . . this obligation attaches to all professionals who have to avoid the stance that problems rest fundamentally with clientele. (31, p. 41)

Summary

In this chapter and in the preceeding ones, the arguments and evidence suggest that when a student fails to profit from the schooling process, a single factor is rarely sufficient to produce the failure. Instead, the factors are multiple and their influence is cumulative, interacting with the unique intellectual and personality predispositions the student brings to the school situation. Failure tends to be the outcome of the school's total impact on the student. For those who fail, the total impact of the school may include one or more of the following: an unwarranted comparison of their performances with the performances of more capable students; nonpromotion; an irrelevant and nonserviceable curriculum; wholly inappropriate classroom teaching strategies; school rules that contain little logic and have as their primary purpose compliance; and prejudice, sarcasm, ridicule and physical abuse. Some students have experienced all of these conditions in the public schools; and for each student, the above conditions over a stretch of years inevitably produce in him the belief that he is incompetent, powerless and needs to remove himself from the school setting.

5

CONDITIONS OF SUCCESSFUL

In the preceding chapters several assumptions and arguments were advanced to describe how schools fail. They have, as their most common characteristic, the school's unwillingness to deal with each learner as a unique person. This chapter describes some of the basic conditions that schools need to provide if each student is to learn and develop in reasonably satisfying ways. These conditions are not all inclusive, nor are they final. They do constitute, however, a very basic blueprint for a realistic psychology of education from which appropriate educational policies and practices may be developed.

PURPOSE AND RESPONSIBILITY OF THE SCHOOL

The primary purpose and responsibility of the school is to provide the necessary conditions for the young to develop the capabilities to think, care and value at advanced levels and to apply these capabilities to improving the human condition. The basic function of education is not to identify for each student a set of truths that he is to take with him throughout his life. Rather, it is to help each student learn how to learn and to adapt to change, how to engage in all that each day holds in a

42

SCHOOL LEARNING

sensitive and open fashion, how to discover and evaluate the new meanings that his environment holds out to him, and how to participate effectively in improving the conditions of society. Education is less than human when information concerning the conditions of man is not drawn into the learning process and when the students' knowledge and skills are not directed toward a constructive change of man's situation. This means that the schools must focus on the individual and his problems, the implications of personal and social philosophies, and the toll that certain current economic and political policies and practices have on people.

We must not prepare the young to become masters of technology if this will make them insensitive to and savage with people and their values. We must not encourage the young to plan for their wealth and their comfort unless they also plan for the elimination of the cruel conditions under which others live. We must not promote freedom unless it means freedom to enhance. We must not tolerate another decade in which people *inhabit,* but do not *live* in, an environment that continually cries out for help. If the schools are to be constructive in their social purpose, they must enable each student to identify with the total human condition; to realize that each man's aspirations, needs and problems are his, and that to infringe on any man's rights is to violate the rights of *all* men; and that any unresolved social problem is partly his responsibility.

In order to assist the young in developing all that is constructive in them and in applying this knowledge to improving the human condition, *each student's capabilities for thinking, caring and valuing must be engaged in an integrated fashion across the entire spectrum of education.* There is a profound interaction of intellectual and emotional characteristics in virtually all forms of human performance. We know, for example, that unless the student is free of extended frustrations, the processes of thinking, reasoning and valuing may be seriously impaired. Equally clear is the fact that unless the basic needs to discover, explore, communicate and experiment are adequately provided for, the student's feeling of achievement, competence and recognition may be compromised. An interdependence of human processes is essential to learn adequately, but this is not the main reason why schools must not fragment educational experiences. The schools must be concerned about providing total involvement for the young primarily because an individual cannot move toward the goal of complete constructive development until all of his learning capabilities are drawn into the educational process in an integrated fashion and applied to issues at all levels of personal and social life.

A school that chooses to promote intellectual development alone risks changing the meaning of rational to insensitive. A school that promotes only the development of feelings risks changing the meaning of sensitive to irrational. Promoting the development of only one level of capabilities in the school restricts the development of human potential and denies the students the skills to deal with *all* of the different kinds of human problems outside the school. Schools must not be centers for intellectual development alone or emotional adjustment alone, but for *human development.*

Schools must see to it that all levels of capabilities are engaged in each of the subject areas. We must not allow each educator to promote the development of one set of capabilities to the exclusion of all other sets. The time has come when the academician, whether he be scientist, mathematician, philosopher or artist, must relate his subject matter to all of the student's learning and behaving levels. He should not focus only on the student's reasoning capabilities or only on his valuing tendencies. Whatever a student studies, drama, physics or economics, *all* of his major learning and behaving processes must be engaged. The objective is to bring the entire scope of each academic discipline and all of the student's constructive capabilities to bear on enhancing the personal life of each student and on improving the conditions of human existence.

INDIVIDUALIZATION OF THE LEARNING PROCESS

Teachers will be successful in helping the young learn and develop in personally and socially advantageous ways when all dimensions of the learning process are individualized for each student. Often the concept of *individualization* is used by the schools to mean that each student may study at his own pace. However, genuine individualization of learning conditions does not refer solely to the *rate* of instruction or learning. The goals to be achieved, the content and processes to be engaged, the psychological climate in which one works, the amount of time to achieve goals, and the criteria for determining achievement, *all* need to be individualized for each student. If only one of these conditions is provided, successful learning, if it occurs, will be short lived. For example, if the schools individualized the *rate of instruction,* but the content is viewed by the learners as dull and meaningless, any improvement in students' performances is likely to be temporary. Trivia or irrelevant material, regardless of the pace at which it is presented, will not result in meaningful learning. The case is the same with each of the other necessary conditions for learning.

The teacher's basic task in providing individualized learning conditions is to start where the learner is in his capabilities, attitudes, concerns and style of learning. No two students come to a learning situation or classroom with the same kind of skills and knowledge. In some instances at least half of the students in a particular class may be capable of obtaining a perfect score on an achievement test before the "necessary" instruction is provided. The students may have had the material previously or they may have picked up the knowledge and skills on their own. Many students, however, may *not* have the prerequisites to undertake and achieve satisfactorily the objectives that are being considered. If the gap between a student's current capabilities and the capabilities he needs to have is too great to undertake a particular program of study, the school should help each learner set realistic goals by beginning precisely where the learner is in his current performance capabilities. Schools must begin with what the student brings to the class rather than with the goals and activities that the school has preselected for him. The case is well stated by Friedenberg.

> To reach the dropouts and give them a reason for staying, the school would have to start by accepting their *raison d'etre*. It would have to take lower-class life seriously as a condition and a pattern of experience, not just as a contemptible and humiliating set of circumstances that every decent boy or girl is anxious to escape from. It would have

to accept their language, their dress, and their values as a *point of departure* . . . not as a trick for luring them into the middle class, but as a way of helping them to explore the meaning of their own lives. This is the way to encourage and nurture potentialities from whatever social class. (9, p. 24)

No goals can be relevant, no processes can be engaged in meaningfully unless they relate to precisely where the student is in his predispositions to learn.

Just as every individual has different preferences for food, clothes and activities, he likewise has his personal learning style, whether it pertains to reading, working with numbers, putting puzzles together, or working with paints. Each student differs in his tempo of responding, some are reflective, others are impulsive; each student differs in his need for structure, some are anxious, others are compulsive, and still others are both; each student differs in his need for direction, some are dependent, others are independent; and each student differs in his capacity to persevere at a task, some give up rather quickly while others persist until the task is completed. We can ignore these and the many other kinds of individual differences that profoundly influence whether or not students perform successfully; we can require all students to follow a predetermined course of study and to complete it within a specified period of time; we can judge each student's efforts and progress against a single criterion; and in so doing we will frustrate each student's efforts to learn and develop in personally advantageous ways.

If we fail to individualize conditions across all dimensions of the learning process, we run the risk of teaching the student only to avoid and escape, whenever possible, what the school has to offer him. If, however, we take into account the student's interests, goals and style of giving and taking in an activity, we will provide the best chance for each student to participate creatively in all that he encounters and to find for himself a greater reward than merely being competent.

FREEDOM AND RESPONSIBILITY OF THE LEARNER

The learner will engage in self-directed learning and demonstrate responsible behavior when he is free to choose from available learning opportunities and when he is held accountable for his choices. If an individual is to help solve, rather than add to, the problems which face man, he must acquire the capabilities to adapt to the reality of continual change. He must learn how to identify personal and social problems and issues, collect and evaluate the evidence, and continually make decisions from a wide range of plausible alternatives. It may be inferred, that each student must play a major role in determining the direction and quality of his education to develop the kind of self-directedness and responsibility for learning that is desirable. Students learn how to make realistic decisions and complete activities independently and responsibly when they are given the *opportunity* to engage in the goal-planning and decision-making processes. They learn democracy when they engage in the democratic process. They become self-disciplined when they are given opportunities to commit themselves to activities they value. The teacher cannot expect the student to make a commitment unless the student is granted the opportunity to choose from among mutually acceptable alternatives. The student is not to be blamed for his unwillingness to accept the responsibility for his own learning when the goals to be achieved and the processes of learning have been *imposed* upon him. A person cannot be expected to commit himself to something he does not choose or value; to do so would require him to falsify his interests, his feelings, and his behavior. *Acceptance of responsibility can be required only when the learner has a major and consistent role in choosing the direction and quality of his own learning and development.*

When students freely select the goals and processes of learning, they must be held accountable for their selections. If the capability to engage in self-directed learning is to be successfully developed, the student must not be excused from his choices or learning contract. It must be made clear to students that free choice is conditional; with the power to decide his goals and select his tasks and materials, there is responsibility for his choices. The same point may be made with regard to school rules; each student is to participate in the establishment of rules, but once the rules have been established, the student is obligated to abide by them. If he fails to uphold the terms of either contract, he runs the risk of having the opportunity to be a participant on his own terms revoked.

LEARNING AS A PERSONAL PROCESS

Successful teachers take into account the fact that meaningful learning is a highly personal process, a function of the individual learner's style of receiving and processing communications. The learning process for each individual is a continuing personal one of acquiring, clarifying, interpreting and synthesizing meanings from his encounters and interactions with ideas, people and events. What others say and do and what they believe to be true and good are meaningful to an individual only insofar as they can be related to *his* experience, to the meanings *he* has extracted from his daily encounters. In short, what and how a student learns is a private and personal matter.

Teachers fail to realize that the kind of meaning a student retains reflects his own life style. Teachers believe that because they see a clear and unmistakable meaning in an event, situation, symbol or idea, their students will also acquire a similar, if not identical, meaning. Often teachers are unaware that many of the concepts which comprise much of our education are concepts whose objective meaning is objective only in the mind of the teacher. The meanings that they wish to convey to students often have no logical basis, but are dependent solely on the experience or point of view of the teacher. *The teacher must continually bear in mind that a communication is given meaning neither by the sender nor by the medium, but by the individual who receives the communication.* Certainly, the content received depends both on the sender and the medium, for they control the quality and quantity of transmission. However, what is perceived depends on the unique dispositions of the receiver. The meaning that a person acquires depends on whether or not he views both the communication and communicator as being credible and personally relevant. It depends also on the person's style of perceiving and processing information, his ability to look at new and different ideas in a nondefensive manner, and his needs for affiliation, power and achievement.

We have all attended brillant, stimulating, thought-provoking lectures, and we have attended some that have been dull, boring, and meaningless. The same applies to group discussions and other processes of learning. It is not the lectures, group discussion, discovery experience, or group encounter that is the heart of the message, it is what the individual participant perceives in the process—confusion, emphasis on the insignificant, or a challenging and constructive interaction of ideas and people. *The medium is not the message, what each learner believes is happening is the message.* This generalization makes it imperative that teachers value the meanings that students acquire rather than the meanings they are expected to acquire. The teacher must not be a director of verbal games or a manipulator of words, but a person who provides assistance to students in discovering and clarifying the meanings that words, ideas, personal interactions and events have for them.

By saying that learning is highly personal, this should not be construed to mean that no attempt should be made to have the learner communicate his meanings to others. Much of the breakdown in human relationships is traceable specifically to a failure to identify and discuss the private meanings that people hold. Personal meanings must be exchanged with others if interactions are to be constructive and if personal and social problems are to be resolved. This means that a major task of the school is to provide conditions which enable each learner to communicate his meanings to others and to measure his ideas against the available evidence.

FREEDOM TO COMMUNICATE

The student will communicate his meanings honestly to others when he believes that he is free to communicate them on his own terms. Each student feels very strongly about the accuracy and meanings of his observations, even though his perceptions may be at odds with the views that others hold. When confronted with the interpretations of others he may try to impose his views on them in an effort to be reassured that he is not in error. He often becomes defensive if his interpretations are attacked. When he feels threatened by the judgments of others, he may become unwilling to share his ideas and feelings. Moreover, he will refrain from communicating his views honestly until he feels that a comfortable and safe climate prevails in his interactions with the teacher and other students.

If the student keeps his beliefs to himself, there is, of course, no opportunity for either the learner or his group to measure his views against the available evidence. It may be inferred that if a person is to express what he really believes, he needs to feel that he can trust others not to prejudge him, manipulate or use him. He needs to feel that he is not required to conform to the values stressed by the school; that he can hold ideas, attitudes and values different from those of the teacher; that he can make mistakes and not be viewed as a failure; and that he can exercise his basic freedom of thought and expression and not be penalized. He needs to feel that he can communicate on his own terms.

PURPOSE DICTATES PROCESS

The appropriateness of particular teaching procedures is a function of the goals to be achieved and the response styles of the learner. Although it seems rather obvious that *how* ones sets out to achieve a goal is largely dependent upon the *kind of goal* to be achieved, teachers fail to see the desirability of using specific teaching methods only in specific situations.

Many teachers employ a single procedure regardless of the goal to be achieved. For example, many teachers will lecture to students, emphasize detail and require memorization although the specific goals and purposes are for students to become creative and independent thinkers. Teachers often fail to realize that the major reason a particular teaching technique is effective is because it is applicable to a specific set of goals. Teaching techniques are not effective or ineffective per se. Their effectiveness is contingent upon their applicability to the situation in question.

The appropriateness of a learning procedure or process is also dependent upon the response styles of the learner. Some students prefer small discussion type classes, while other students prefer to work alone, and still others work optimally in a large group. For students who learn more effectively in groups, the *structure* of the group is important. Some students learn more effectively in a group comprised of individuals who are similar in their rates of learning and who have similar goals to achieve, while others learn optimally in a group comprised of students who have different goals and different rates and styles of learning. It is clear that one of the basic tasks of the teacher is to identify and provide for each student the materials, direction and kind of classroom interaction that is most appropriate for him to achieve his particular goals. To do this adequately, the teacher needs to make available to students optional, but equally acceptable learning opportunities. He also needs to provide students with a range of learning processes from which they may choose, e.g., student-student assistance and independent study.

JOINT EVALUATION

Evaluation is an integral part of the learning process and it must actively involve both the teacher and student. In order to plan appropriate learning opportunities for the student, the teacher must first identify the student's current performance capabilities. In fact, the teacher needs to gather and interpret information about a student's performance capabilities *before, during* and *after* each instructional decision to make accurate judgments about the most appropriate learning conditions for the student. This makes it clear that evaluation is not something apart from learning. It is central to the learning enterprise, and it is continuous.

A second important point to note about evaluation is that to have each student develop the skills to engage in self-directed learning, the student will need to assume a major and consistent role in the evaluation of his work. This means that the student must be provided with conditions which enable him to look objectively at his progress and behavior. He must be provided with opportunities to identify and establish valid criteria of achievement, to gather the available evidence, and to make judgments concerning the acceptability of his own work. This should not be interpreted as meaning that the teacher has no role in evaluation. Assuredly, the teacher needs to offer his own judgments about the students' performances. However, his judgments are not imposed on the learner; rather, they are *shared* with him. The teacher says to the student, "Here are my observations about what you have set out to do, how you have tried to reach your goals, and how successful you have been in your efforts." The teacher's task in evaluation is not to *tell* the student how he has or has not measured up to the *teacher's standards*. Instead, his major task is to help the student to acquire the skills to assess for himself the quality and direction of his own learning.

INDIVIDUALIZED CRITERIA OF ACHIEVEMENT

Criteria for evaluating an individual student's performance in a learning program must be based on that student's capabilities, concerns and choices. If we are to establish defensible standards of achievement for each student we must view his performance in terms of the particular goals set for him. The teacher cannot utilize a common course of study and select the *class average* as the minimum acceptable level of performance for *all* students. If he does, the resulting grades which are assigned to students will be unfair. Students below average in ability and motivation would need to perform beyond their capabilities to obtain a passing grade. It is invalid for a teacher to measure a student's performance in relation to the abilities, concerns and choices of *other* students whose *learning predispositions he does not share.* The only defensible basis for determining whether or not a student is successful in his learning efforts is to measure his performance in relation to *his pre-learning behaviors.*

A corollary of the above principle is that *no student is a failure. He may make an unacceptable number of errors, or he may not complete a planned activity, or both. However, he does not fail!* Let me explain. The majority of man's performance capabilities, from simple motor skills to complex problem-solving capabilities, have developed largely as the result of a trial-error-trial-success approach. It may be inferred from this assumption that *error-making is not failure, but a fundamental part of the process of learning.* Consequently, if the rate of error-making prevents a student from achieving his goals within a reasonable period of time, he should not be assigned a failing grade, but rather should be provided with a more appropriate instructional program.

A second point deals with the student's inability or unwillingness to complete a task or program satisfactorily. If a student does not complete the requirements of a program which he has *not* helped to plan, it would be a gross injustice to make *any* judgment about the acceptability of his work. Without freedom there can be no commitment, and without choice there can be no responsibility. When, however, the student does not complete a task or course of study which he and his teacher jointly discuss, plan and agree on, then a statement of his *actual* performance needs to be made.

When we look at a student's poor performance, either he did not complete the entire activity or he exhibited a high rate of error-making, or both. Consequently, a warranted evaluation would include the following: (a) statements describing the satisfactory and unsatisfactory aspects of the student's performance and explaining *why* they are so, (b) either the grade "incomplete" or "no grade," and (c) statements about the particular kinds of learning conditions that would be more appropriate and that would need to be arranged for the student. The student would never be viewed as a *failure,* nor would he be assigned a grade labeling him one.

The notion of failure is used in our schools primarily because the schooling process is woven into the aspects of our social fabric which stress condemnation and punishment rather than a modification of learning conditions when unacceptable behavior patterns are exhibited. However, if we are to be successful in helping our youth develop the best that is in them, we must eliminate the vindictiveness that pervades our public schools. *Failure is not instructive in any educational sense.* It does not facilitate constructive and personally meaningful learning. It always prevents these kinds of learning from taking place and it often destroys the very individuals who most desperately need satisfying educational experiences.

SUMMARY

In this chapter I have discussed what I believe to be some very basic assumptions about successful school learning. 1) Learning opportunities cannot be fragmented if the student is to develop all that is constructive in him and relate this to improving the human condition. 2) The starting point in the educational process is with the student himself —his curiosity to know, his concerns and his styles of learning and developing. 3) Each individual needs to be a participant on his own terms. He must play the central role in the goals selected, the activities encountered and the judgment of his success. He needs to be given the opportunities to choose freely from available alternatives, and he must be held accountable for his choices. In short, the student must be provided with the conditions which allow him to be the instrument of his own development.

In this chapter I did not include a discussion of the role of the inquiry process in learning. I believe that open and thorough inquiry is essential if students are to learn and develop in personally and socially meaningful ways; for this reason the next chapter is devoted entirely to the nature and utilization of inquiry in the classroom.

THE INQUIRY PROCESS

An avowed purpose of American public education is to provide the conditions which enable our youths to learn and develop in personally and socially advantageous ways, thereby helping to solve, rather than adding to, the problems that face man. To achieve this purpose the schools need to provide students with the opportunities to examine freely and thoroughly all of the issues that are before them. Unfortunately, the opportunities to engage in the inquiry process are rarely made available to students. Perkins (39), for example, reports in his research that in the typical elementary school classroom we tend to find 75 per cent of the available time devoted to seat work and only five per cent of the time set aside for discussion. Moreover, only about one per cent of the time is used for asking "thinking" questions and only about four per cent of the time is used for considering the merits of a student's idea or answer.

Why isn't more time set aside for free and open inquiry? One of the major reasons is that teachers assume that their subject areas need to be covered, as comprehensively as possible. When this assumption is put into practice, very little, if any, time is made available for students to ask questions. However, both the assumption and the practice are unwarranted. The available evidence suggests that while each individual

IN LEARNING

needs to acquire the *skills to learn*—to read, speak, write and work with information and symbols, there is no organized body of knowledge which educators agree is essential for all people.

Over 2,000 years ago Aristotle stated in his *Politics:*

> All men do not agree in those things they would have the children learn. From the present mode of education we cannot determine with certainty to which men incline, whether to instruct a child in what will be useful to him in life, or what tends to virtue, or what is excellent, for all these things have their separate defenders. (Book VIII, Chap. 2, par. 1)

The same point could just as well be made today. Can we say with certainty that one kind of knowledge is more important or useful than another to a particular student? Can we know with certainty the kinds of knowledge that a student will need ten years or even five years after he leaves school? When I was in high school I was told that the study of Latin was essential to do well in college and to become a cultured gentleman. Would the case for Latin be argued the same way today? Most of the things that I learned in psychology as an undergraduate are today largely inapplicable and in some respects totally inaccurate.

We have no way of knowing with certainty the knowledge that will be most useful or valuable in the future. This is true because the appropriateness or applicabiltiy of knowledge to the solution of problems is dependent on the unique and changing circumstances that surround each problem. The schools, therefore, do not need to provide each student with increasing amounts of subject matter. Instead, they need to provide students with the opportunities to develop the skills to cope with changing knowledge. Personal and social problems will not be solved by requiring students to assimilate more and more subject matter which will be inapplicable a few years later. They will be solved only when the schools help students learn how to learn and how to analyze and evaluate in an ongoing fashion all that they encounter. When the schools provide these kinds of learning conditions, they are increasing the likelihood that the knowledge students acquire today will not betray them in the future.

A second reason why free and open inquiry is not found to be the core of the learning process in the schools is that most teachers believe that if they encourage freedom of inquiry, students will begin to challenge every aspect of our social order. Many teachers believe that eventually our most cherished values, and perhaps democracy itself, will be destroyed if students are permitted to ask too many questions. It seems to me that when a society has come to a point in its history where it is afraid that an issue cannot withstand honest and thorough examination, then there is all the more reason for promoting inquiry. It is a paradox that many teachers, on the one hand, do not provide students with the opportunities to question and examine issues, and on the other hand, insist that students pay verbal tribute to our democratic heritage and institutions. Their unwillingness to promote free inquiry is strange indeed when we consider that the meaning of freedom to learn is that each student is to be provided with the conditions . . .

> to study and discuss significant moral, scientific, social, economic, and political issues, . . . to have access to a variety of publications and materials that relate to issues studied in class, . . . to study and discuss all sides of the issue in an atmosphere where there can be a give and take on ideas without loss of personal dignity, . . . (and) to teach and express an opinion or hold values that may be different from those of other members of the class and from those of the teacher. (37, pp. 217–219)

Assuredly, if education is viewed as the "transmission of our heritage," rather than as an honest exploration of the meaning of ideas today, then we have reason to shun inquiry. If our defense of policies, practices and values rests not on an open analysis of argument and evidence, but on tradition or authority, then indeed we have reason to be afraid of critical thought itself. However, no respect for a society and its institutions can develop from an uncritical acceptance of their processes. Our history makes it quite clear that no problems can be dealt with adequately unless people engage in a free and thorough examination of the issues involved.

A third argument against open inquiry that teachers present is that students become apprehensive unless they have someone lecture to them or give them the "right" answers. However, we know enough about human learning and development to say that when teachers provide conditions for all students to learn in personally meaningful ways, i.e., accept and value students as individuals and provide them with relevant goals, materials, and systems of evaluation, students become open in their interactions with each other and with teachers. In time they prefer an inquiry approach to an expository approach.

Many students are apprehensive about participating in inquiry classes because . . .

> most of the conditions prevailing in our schools operate against creativity, free discussion of issues, and the genuine motivation to learn. The prevailing grading system, the promotion policies, the subject by subject division of knowledge, the standardized and college entrance examinations, and the general organization and structure of the school usually put severe restraints on a discovery–or inquiry–centered program. (29, p. 251)

Most students are exposed year after year only to a tell and test approach. Some teachers engage in inquiry, but it is often phoney or right answer oriented. Moreover, driven each year by an unrelenting emphasis on competition, students quickly get the message. Top priority must be given to survival, and survival is contingent on coming up with the right answers. Under such "learning" conditions students are going to be very reluctant to discuss their own ideas or engage in an open inquiry process. If students are apprehensive at the outset of the inquiry process, it is because conditions in the schools have *prevented* them from participating freely in open inquiry.

Another point that we often hear teachers make is that children and adolescents are not mature enough to understand. These teachers believe that the young are too impressionable; consequently, they can be easily led astray if we allow them to question our values. Yes, the young are impressionable, but being impressionable means only that they are open—open to new and constructive levels of development or to constricted ways of thinking and behaving. This is precisely why the young need to be provided with the opportunities to identify problems accurately, to state the involved issues, to gather and interpret the relevant evidence, and to discuss and debate the assumptions, conclusions and implications.

If we were to pursue the issue further we could ask, "If people are not mature enough when they are in school, when do people become mature in their judgment?" Do they become mature after they leave school? I don't believe that anyone who has listened to adults argue with one another and with children, or observed our political parties and convention delegates select a person who will eventually become President of the United States, can say that the young have a monopoly on immature behavior. When it comes to a sensitivity to human problems, a concern about their implications, and a dedication to their resolution, young people are in the forefront. I believe that the real reason why teachers give phoney reasons for not permitting free and open inquiry is evident. They are afraid! They are afraid that when the issues are raised the right answer will not be selected by students, or worse yet, no right answer may be even perceived by them. They are afraid that students may see only alternatives that are more or less valid, moral or plausible.

A response style that many teachers adopt to deal with their fears that the correct answer will not be selected is to utilize strategies which demand intellectual compliance. In order to elicit compliance, teachers often take behaviors or concepts which have very different meanings and insist to students that they are equivalent in meaning. For example, teachers equate disagreement with disloyalty, or democracy with the fixed set of beliefs that they hold. By suggesting to students that they may be disloyal when they disagree with the right answer, teachers hope to encourage students to conform, or at least be silent. What teachers and administrators too often do in today's schools is

> . . . impugn the loyalty of those who dissent, raise questions, or otherwise refuse to be cast in a mold. Some of these "superpatriots" are sincere and conscientious but uninformed persons; others serve groups whose vested interests are endangered by free inquiry. Their efforts result in book purges, loyalty oaths, curriculum restrictions, and other too familiar interferences with freedom to teach and freedom to learn. (30, p. 489)

The "loyalty–demands–conformity" strategy is easy to spot. All open and honest inquiry is rejected, whether the issue be freedom, competition, foreign policy or civil rights. It is rejected because it inevitably leads to inquiry into the purpose, value and conditions of loyalty itself.

It is time the schools acknowledged that one of the basic purposes of the educational process is to have each individual examine all of the important assumptions and values before him and to determine if they apply to current conditions, measure up against the evidence, and are constructive to the development of man. If they fail to meet these criteria, their affirmation is indefensible and should not be required.

If the young are to acquire the wisdom, versatility and grace needed to cope with reality outside the school, and if democracy is indeed to survive, opportunities must be made available for each person to explore freely and honestly the world he has before him and the person he has the potentiality to become. To be sure, much about the destiny of man and the nature of the democratic process can be learned from great writings of the past and present, however, the most appropriate and relevant opportunities for the young to engage in personally and socially constructive learning are the encounters with contemporary issues that can be provided in the classroom every day.

WHEN INQUIRY IS PHONEY

Although the world in which we live is an uncertain one with few uncomplicated answers to problems, the schools tend to convey the notion that each problem has a clear and simple answer. Often what is purported to be a free and open discussion is nothing more than a manipulations of questions, phrases and words until the teacher-preferred or "correct" answer is given.

The teacher often has a list of questions that he asks students and a set of sequential statements that he uses to get students to zero in on the answers that are acceptable to him. I am not arguing against the use of questions or sequential statements designed to assist a student in perceiving a number of plausible relationships among ideas. What I am protesting is the use of questions or statements carefully designed to deceive the student into thinking that there is only one acceptable answer in each instance—an answer that happens to be identical to the one held by the teacher.

A number of writers, including Holt and Leacock, find that this practice of deceptive questioning is widespread in the schools. Some teachers try to elicit from students not only the correct meaning, but also *specific words*, even though several different words would convey essentially the same meaning the teacher is looking for. *Children are even denied the use of their own words to convey to the teacher the meaning he wants.* One instance of this practice is reported by Leacock who observed a poetry class.

> T: You read poetry for your . . .?
> Child: Enjoyment.
> T: What else?
> Another Child: Entertainment.
> T: Yes, another word?
> Marcia: Recreation.
> T: Yes, but what does it make you feel?
> Roger: Good.
> T: Yes, it's good for you, and don't you also read it for *pleasure*?
> T writes the word "pleasure" on the board . . . (26, p. 52)

The above incident is not an uncommon one. Under the guise of open discussion the teacher asks more and more pointed questions until the specific word or answer he is looking for comes out. He then writes it on the board to make sure every student sees that it is indeed the correct response. He will then proceed to explain to students why it is so.

Many teachers have no conception of the nature of a genuinely honest discussion.

> "I ask the leading question to get the answer that I want," said a teacher when discussing "experience charts." "As we are discussing, I will put down the main thoughts of what I want to go down on the chart. They enjoy that. They like to talk. They enjoy discussion . . . ." (26, p. 51)

So many teachers do not realize that in an honest discussion each participant must be free to raise the questions that he believes are important, to express the feelings and ideas he values, and to suggest the conclusions or solutions that seem most plausible to him. Inquiry is phoney when personally meaningful and socially important issues are not raised, when answers to questions reflect the teacher's preference and when students' perceptions are excluded from the learning process. To achieve the goal of assisting each individual to develop all that is constructive in him and relate this to the human condition, the school must provide the learner with the opportunity to engage in open and genuine inquiry. School must be a place where each student can probe any issue about man and his environment and determine whether or not a principle of conduct, a statement of causality, or a solution to personal and social problems is based on evidence and persuasive argument.

PREREQUISITES TO HONEST INQUIRY

In order to have a genuine and thorough examination of ideas and values occur in the school, we need to have an issue-centered curriculum. The curriculum should be issue-centered in the sense that man's basic concerns should be the guiding principles in determining subject matter for consideration. In such a curriculum, problems and concerns are not molded to fit traditionally defined fields of study; instead, subject concepts feed into issues. Concepts, principles and theories are drawn from any established academic discipline that can aid in the examination of problems and in the resolution of the issues in question.

The structure of an issue-centered curriculum is not along the lines of traditionally separate fields of study because it cannot be established along the lines of traditionally separate fields of study and still be applicable to the multi-dimensional problems we face. The nature of effective personal and social problem solving is such that we must cut across traditionally separate fields of study in order to identify and resolve problems satisfactorily. An issue-centered curriculum is structured in the sense that priority is given to contemporary problems and to the needs, concerns and learning styles of students. Mazzialas and Zevin (29) report from their research with high school students that the latter notion of structure is necessary if personally meaningful and socially important learning is to take place. They find in their research on students' handling of social problems that . . .

> as students got involved in discussions of graft, bad Samaritanism, racial intermarriage, and foreign policy, they employed knowledge and analytical methods from social science, psychology, art, history, law, jurisprudence, philosophy, and science, and they capitalized on their own experiences and views of society and the prevailing ethical code. Had the class remained within the traditional confines of subject matter specialization and differentiation, it would never have explored the foregoing value-permeated and controversial topics. (29, p. 261)

Not only do we need to break down the boundaries of traditionally separate subject areas, but we also need to realize that there is no structure of organized knowledge outside the mind of the knower. Although academicians speak of "bodies of knowledge," to the learner, knowledge structures often appear artificial. The structures of knowledge that are presented in the school often make sense only to the subject-matter specialists. Teachers must realize that although they view arrangements of words as concepts and principles, words become meaningful to the learner only when *he* attaches meaning to them; and his own needs, concerns and learning style will dictate what the meanings will be. The knowledge that each learner actually possesses is an individual mosaic of ideas—an individual synthesis of the perceptions that *he* has acquired.

It may be inferred that a realistic curriculum is also a student-oriented one. It needs to be student-oriented in the sense that students, with the help of the teacher, select the issues and problems that are to be considered. The teacher's role as a "planner" is largely that of a person who suggests topics—their importance and implications—and clarifies the available optional learning activities—activities which take into account the problems we face, the reservoir of knowledge to which we have access, and the concerns that students express. Beyond that the teacher suggests materials, provides some of his own materials, organizes the topics, establishes times for inquiry, and assists students in their investigation of the issues.

THE FACILITATION OF GROUP INQUIRY

Inquiry may take place in an interpersonal form (e.g., group inquiry, group encounter, and role playing) or in an individual form (e.g., programmed learning and individually perscribed instruction). While both forms of learning are valuable, I am inclined to believe that the more advantageous form of inquiry occurs in the group. The basic reason is that the kind of reality in which we find ourselves and the kinds of issues and problems that need to be resolved require an interdependence of people. Unfortunately, the present tendency in our schools is to move more and more toward the use of processes which *decrease* rather than increase the amount of interaction between people.

To be sure, when the student works alone, as he does with programmed learning, he can acquire factual knowledge, perceive some relationships among ideas and determine how certain things tend to happen when certain conditions are present. The student can also work at his own rate and receive frequent and useful information about the adequacy of his responses. On the deficit side, programmed learning frequently presents fragmented information rather than interrelated concepts and principles as they apply to problem solving. It does not provide for a complete treatment of the nature of the problem solving process. Programmed learning also minimizes, and perhaps precludes, the communication of meanings between students and has the effect of isolating students from one another. Programmed learning and other individual approaches to learning may be of optimum use when integrated into a program where interpersonal processes are central. A student can perhaps engage in inquiry most effectively when individualized processes are utilized to supplement interpersonal approaches.

Getting Started

Most students come to class believing that they are not expected to communicate directly with anyone in the class except the teacher. Often they are reluctant to communicate even with the teacher because in the past they have been criticized or made to feel incompetent when they expressed their views. Consequently, to have students become participants, teachers need to create a climate that students perceive as being psychologically safe and one in which participation is expected.

Encouraging Participation

The likelihood that all students will participate meaningfully in an interpersonal inquiry process is small if they cannot see each other face to face. When students are unable to look directly at other members of a group they are inclined to feel less involved and therefore less important to the interactions that may take place in class. Consequently, a seating arrangement which encourages verbal and nonverbal communication among all members of the group is best. The circle formation is an ideal arrangement for creating at least a direct visual line of communication with each individual.

The first class meeting is a good time for the teacher and each member of the class to find out who is in the group—to exchange names, interests, ambitions, and important personal experiences. This encourages students to feel that the group may be important to them and that they may find it to their advantage to become active participants.

Each group should be kept small—18 to 20 members at the most. If the class is large, the teacher will need to divide the students into smaller groups after the students become acquainted and after the topics for investigation have been planned. The reason for small groups is simple, an intensive and thorough examination of issues and problems is difficult with large groups. To be sure, inquiry can take place when a single group has as many as 35 participants, but, the teacher must keep in mind that for each participant there is a viewpoint and a set of feelings which come into play when each issue is raised. The larger the group, the more viewpoints and feelings expressed; therefore, the longer it takes the group to resolve an issue. This in turn reduces the number of issues that may be examined in the course of a semester. Admittedly, not every student will actively communicate his feelings and ideas to others, regardless of the size of the group. However, each person needs to feel that if he wants to contribute he has the opportunity to do so.

The second meeting of the group may be set aside for planning the topics to be investigated and the time to be allotted for each topic. The teacher can implement open discussion of the concerns of the students and the topics which are related to the subject by distributing to students a list of the topics that he believes pertain to his field of study. He and the students can then take each topic on the list and individually accept, modify or reject it. Every effort should be made for students to create original topics. The final list of topics selected should reflect both the teacher's and students' best efforts to combine areas of investigation which they believe to be personally relevant and socially important. A decision concerning both the order in which the topics will be examined and the amount of time set aside for the initial investigation of each topic may also be dealt with during the second session.

Often students are divided on some of the topics they wish to investigate. In these situations one or two multiple topic sessions may be planned with the topics and their respective subgroups scheduled for the same inquiry session. The teacher then moves from group to group to assist students in their investigations. It is advisable not to have a multiple topic session until at least two or three other topics have been examined. This gives students some opportunities to develop an awareness of some of the procedures that they need to follow to examine their topics effectively.

A useful way of preparing for each separate inquiry session is to make accessible in advance of the session sets of reading materials, taped lectures, laboratory demonstrations, reference works, and films pertinent to the topic to be considered. This approach has two distinct advantages; each student has an opportunity to come in contact with a variety of information sources and reference points on which to base a discussion, and students are not on the spot to draw on a single text or on their experiences in other courses to participate effectively. They feel more comfortable when they have had recent and optional experiences that touch directly on the issue or problem.

A Psychologically Safe Climate

It is important that students perceive from the very outset of the course that their individual interpretations and feelings are valued and sought and that the teacher will not pass judgment on the correctness of a response. Therefore, questions should be exploratory in nature, eliciting students' personal impressions, rather than requiring specific answers. Questions, such as, "What did you find interesting in the readings?" or "How meaningful were the situations in the film to your personal life?" are exploratory in nature rather than judgmental. This approach is important to follow also because of the relationship between feeling and thinking. There are two kinds of meaning that may be perceived by an individual—meaning on a feeling level and meaning on a thinking level.

The two levels of meaning are distinctly different, yet interdependent when dealing with the resolution of issues. Comprehensive inquiry into issues cannot proceed freely and openly unless the meanings at the feeling level, which students perceive as threatening, are handled first.

The specific kinds of feelings that inhibit or prevent the exchange of intellectual meanings are those which arise when an individual senses that his beliefs and values may be attacked or ridiculed. For example, if a student has strong negative feelings toward members of minority groups, he is quite likely to feel threatened on being asked to accept the proposition "each person should have equal right and access to the educational conditions he needs to learn and develop." Rogers (44), points out, however, that ideas or views which are threatening to an individual are more likely to be explored and assimilated when a climate for self-initiated change is provided. When a student regards himself as being in an environment which is accepting and supportive and when he becomes convinced that his most cherished values and basic beliefs are not in any real danger, he is more likely to examine the intellectual meanings that ideas may hold for him. This means that from the outset of the inquiry process, the teacher needs to assure each student that his grade will not depend on a change in his attitudes or values. Change on his part is an option that he is free to accept or reject at any time.

To get feelings out into the open the teacher needs first to accept whatever expression a student communicates. (44) Accepting each individual's feelings and values does not mean that the teacher agrees with them. It means instead that the teacher views each individual as being of value and that the student's worth is not contingent upon having attitudes and ideas acceptable to the teacher or other members of the group. A nod of the head or a comment, such as, "I see," may convey acceptance. Any kind of contributory response by a group member, whether it be a sigh, smile or sign of irritation, should be acknowledged by the teacher with an accepting gesture or comment. This acknowledgement may suggest to the student that his response is accepted, and this in turn may encourage him to participate verbally.

Everyone knows that there is some risk involved in being in a group, therefore, if each student is to participate freely, he needs to feel that the teacher will not pass judgment on the quality of his participation or the lack of it. Each student needs to believe that the teacher can be trusted not to criticize, ridicule or belittle him. Consequently, the teacher should never show in word or behavior that he finds a student's grammar, choice of words, or mannerisms different. Each student is struggling to communicate what is part of himself, and for the teacher to judge his language or behavior as inadequate or inferior is to risk destroying his willingness to participate and his belief that he has something of value to offer.

Another practice which encourages open communication of feelings is for the teacher to *reflect* what the students are saying. (44) A useful way of reflecting feelings is for the teacher to restate a student's ideas in his own words and then ask the student if his restatement is essentially accurate. This procedure also serves to check whether or not the same perceptions and meanings were acquired by the other members of the group.

When there is the likelihood that a student may feel threatened by an idea or value that has been expressed by other group members, it is advisable to ask him how he *feels* about the idea rather than whether he *agrees* with it. Let the student determine for himself what he wants to contribute. Don't put him in a position where he feels that a right answer needs to be given. The art of keeping threats at a low level rests essentially on the skill of asking questions which convey a desire to understand. Examples of such questions would be the following: "Could you elaborate on that a little more?" "How may that recommendation be applied to our situation?" "Do you believe that this suggestion would solve the entire problem or just some aspects of it?" "Would a different approach to the problem be more effective?" "What may be some of the implications of this plan for each person's behavior?" "What might be some of the workable aspects of that suggestion?"

Checking Progress

It is necessary for the teacher to check from time to time where students believe they are in their investigation of the issue under consideration. A useful procedure may be to summarize before and after each inquiry session the basic points made to date on the current issue. Summaries may serve four valuable functions. They may enable the group to check the meanings that have been communicated to see whether or not there is a fairly accurate understanding of what has been said and settled. The teacher may ask, for example, "Before we go any further, let me see if I can restate what has been said." In his restatements the teacher should reflect both the feelings and the intellectual meanings that have been expressed. The teacher would then ask the group to comment on the accuracy of his summary.

Summaries improve communication and increase participation within the group. A single set of words may communicate one meaning to one student and an entirely different meaning to other students. Consequently, a summary may suggest a disagreement about the meanings perceived in an earlier discussion. If disagreements are carefully handled, they may improve the quality of communication among the group's current participants and also bring students into a discussion who heretofore were reluctant to communicate.

Summaries also serve to sharpen each individual member's skills for thinking critically about the issues. A summary makes it possible for students to examine simultaneously the evidence presented both for and against a point of view, to make progressively finer distinctions among words, meanings and arguments, and to clarify, reconsider or modify their previously expressed views.

Finally, summaries help the group separate the resolved issues from the unresolved ones and this lessens the likelihood of rediscussing settled issues in upcoming inquiry sessions. The teacher can communicate the progress made by listing the issues that have been resolved or temporarily set aside, and noting where there is agreement and disagreement in the group. (28)

Involving All Members

Inquiry sessions often have a tendency to involve only a few group members consistently in an exchange of ideas. To spread participation, the teacher should utilize procedures which encourage all members of the group to make a contribution. Some of the following procedures may be effective for this purpose: (28)

1. Check with the entire group to determine where agreement and disagreement lie with respect to a recently stated idea. The instructor might ask, "How do you as a group feel about this?" or, "Do all of you feel the same way about this idea?" If the teacher receives simple "yes" or "no" responses he might add, "Well, let's examine some of the dimensions and implications of this view, because I didn't intend to convey to you that this is a simple matter."*

2. After questions are submitted to the group, allow long pauses or follow a question with a statement, such as, "Let's think about this for a minute." Occasionally teachers, including myself, make the mistake of either beginning to supply responses to their own questions or changing the question when students seem to be "taking too long" to respond. However, the long pause is needed to allow each student is to have ample time to think about the question, and plan some kind of response.

There are three major reasons why it is not advisable to call on individual students for the purpose of spreading participation. First, the individual may feel on the spot to come up with, not only a response, but an acceptable one; he may feel that when he is requested to say something he is being asked to run the risk of appearing foolish or saying something that others may criticize. Second, when the teacher requires an individual student to participate and the student feels that he does not have anything meaningful that he would like to share with the other group members, he may perceive the purpose of the inquiry sessions as participation for the sake of participation. Even if the teacher does induce a reluctant student to speak, the student quite likely will not speak freely and honestly. Third, when a teacher calls on an individual student, the other group members may interpret the teacher's behavior as favoritism of the students selected and rejection of the students not selected.

Stepping Up Critical Thinking

After a number of inquiry sessions have taken place and students have developed considerable trust in the teacher and confidence in themselves, the teacher can begin to press students to engage more thoroughly in a defense of their statements, to engage more strongly in debate, and to face their own feelings and beliefs. For example, the teacher can probe whether or not a student's argument for his views is a rationalization or a genuinely honest reason. An example of a teacher's statement which requires the student to defend his position is, "I think I understand what you are saying, however, I can't seem to reconcile your position with the fact that. . . ." It must be made clear, however, that an emphasis on debate and confrontation should not be encouraged until the sessions are far enough along that students do not feel threatened by questions which demand more evidence, or questions which probe how each student feels personally about an issue. *At all times* the teacher must be cautious about his use of questions; the trust that often takes so long to develop in interpersonal inquiry can be quickly chipped away by careless probing.

In facilitating inquiry through confrontation, the teacher prods students about the defensibility and implications of their responses, but he does not establish his own views as guidelines in considering defensible answers. His basic responsibility in the discussion is to keep students on the issue, question assumptions that they make and have them substantiate their statements. The interaction is primarily a dialectical exchange of ideas. When the student directs a question toward the teacher, the teacher redirects the question to the student. In the event that a student persists in wanting the teacher to state his views, the teacher should determine if the student is trying to escape the responsibility of providing his own answers or if the students wishes to consider other proposed solutions to problems. When the teacher suspects the former he could pose to the student a question, such as, "Do you think each individual needs to come up with the answer himself?" If, however, the student is asking either for information that may be available only to the teacher or for a clarification of an earlier statement, then the teacher would answer the student's question without either leading the student to a conclusion or implying that his response is a guideline for the student to follow in forming an answer.

When a student accepts an answer or solution, the teacher's role is to require the student to present the supporting evidence and to establish the conditions under which his conclusion is believed valid or defensible. When no valid conclusion can be drawn, the teacher and the students need to briefly review their statements of the problem, their methods of seeking a solution, and the evidence they have gathered. Often this kind of reexamination of the inquiry process helps to suggest a plausible solution or a new method of attack to arrive at a solution.

Occasionally, the inability to arrive at a warranted conclusion is the result of disagreements which may develop because one or more students feel either threatened by the views of others or inclined to view issues and answers as "either–or" types of situations, rather than "conditional–relative" ones. One approach for dealing with disagreements is to identify and list the divergent points of view. If, for example, the interpretations tend to fall into one of two categories, the arguments or views may be listed as favoring either Premise 1 or Premise 2, or they may be stated as being for or against a particular conclusion. The teacher should present the different points as representing two philosophical positions rather than a disagreement between two students. This will minimize the chance that a student will be placed in the position of becoming a loser. If students wish to debate the arguments for each premise, perhaps further research is called for, and some time should be set aside for it.

The teacher himself is likely to feel threatened when the students with whom he is having an open exchange of ideas express beliefs or values that are diametrically opposed to his. He may very much like to have them see things the way he does. Perhaps he may even wish to preach to them and have them come over to his point of view. However, he needs to ask himself if he is sure of the defensibility of his beliefs. Perhaps the greatest challenge to a teacher is for him to cast his own views into the arena of analysis and argument and have the group debate their worth. He, more than anybody else, must face up to the fact that no idea is immune from critical analysis. No truth or fact may be held as defensible except in terms of the evidence that is available.

It is extremely difficult for a teacher whose views are challenged to refrain from drawing conclusions for students, yet refrain he must. However, he may clarify students' assumptions, arguments and conclusions and recast them in the form of questions to have students consider additional evidence or to consider their implications. But, if students can provide no adequate answer or solution, the teacher cannot propose one for them. The issue must remain unresolved, although a decision should be made by the students either to research the issue until resolved, or to set it aside for the present and consider other issues. No issue should be closed until the students have arrived at a resolution that is persuasive in their minds, or unless they have agreed that no more meaningful progress can be made on the issue.

SUMMARY

In this chapter I discussed the importance of free and open inquiry to constructive learning. I described one approach, group inquiry, and suggested a number of guidelines that may facilitate this form of inquiry in the classroom. The basic purpose of the group inquiry process is to provide students with the conditions (a) to acquire the capabilities they need to deal with changing knowledge, (b) to develop a sensitivity to the issues and problems that face man, and (c) to value the need to participate actively in improving the human condition. The specific topics for investigation are jointly determined by students and teacher with organizational assistance provided by the teacher. Inquiry takes place across all dimensions of the students' response capabilities—thinking, feeling, caring and valuing. Appreciating the role that feelings and attitudes play in acquiring and utilizing intellectual skills, the teacher endeavors to provide a climate of psychological safety—an environment in which each individual feels free to express his own views. He asks exploratory questions rather than judgmental ones, and he accepts and reflects students' responses. As students develop increasingly more trust in the teacher and confidence in themselves as competent problem solvers, the teacher asks more probing questions which require students to present a strong defense of their statements, and face their own attitudes and behavior. Each student is asked to reexamine his initial views in the light of new evidence, to question assumptions which present little supportive evidence, and to refrain from drawing conclusions or settling on solutions until persuasive evidence and arguments have been presented. The teacher continually emphasizes that there are no right or wrong, good or bad answers, only valid, defensible or plausible ones.

I noted the opposition to having open inquiry in the school and stressed the fact that many conditions exist in the schools which prevent inquiry from taking place. It was emphasized that students cannot develop the skills to think critically about contemporary issues and to care about the implications of social policies and practices from one course or in a single semester. Free and open inquiry must pervade all dimensions of the educational process; for this to occur, substantive reform must take place in the purpose and organization of the schools, in the schools' philosophy of human learning, and in the content and processes that are arranged for each student.

7

CHARACTERISTICS OF

In the two preceding chapters a number of conditions were proposed as being essential for each student to learn and develop in personally and socially constructive ways. These conditions, when viewed together, suggest a teaching model. This model requires: first, that we identify where the student is in all of his relevant predispositions to learn and develop; second, that we assist the student in planning goals that are appropriate and meaningful to him—in terms of *his* learning predispositions; third, that we assist the student in the selection of appropriate materials and activities, knowing that processes are valid only in terms of the goals to be achieved and the learning styles of the student; fourth, that we provide a climate in which inquiry may take place in an open and constructive fashion, and in which there is acceptance of responsibility for jointly established rules of behavior; and fifth, that we assist the student in evaluating his own work, knowing that a concept of achievement and a system of evaluation are defensible only in terms of the student's unique starting points, the goals planned by him and the processes of learning in which he engages.

This is a basic teaching model. This teaching model in turn suggests many of the capabilities that the teacher himself must possess to provide appropriate learning conditions. It is these capabilities that are our concern in this chapter.

THE COMPETENT TEACHER

CHARACTERISTICS OF A COMPETENT TEACHER

Available research and clinical evidence regarding meaningful learning and effective teaching suggest that a competent teacher is characterized by the following: 1) he can engage students in an open and trusting relationship by his capacity to listen and accept; 2) he is skilled in the use of different diagnostic, planning, facilitative and evaluative procedures and is knowledgeable about their limitations; 3) he is experimental in his general attitude toward identifying and providing appropriate learning conditions; and 4) he can look at his own beliefs, feelings and behavior openly and can find ways to make them more constructive to himself and others. (3, 4, 16, 27, 44)

He can engage students in an open and trusting relationship by his capacity to listen and accept

Listening. When the teacher listens competently to what a student is saying, he hears not only the student's words, but his feelings and meanings. Sensitive listening is a perception of and a responsiveness to the student's view of reality.

Rogers points out that when there is sensitive listening to the meanings that are being communicated, the individual who is heard often perceives himself and his reality differently.

> When I do truly hear a person . . . not simply his words, but *him*, and when I let him know that I have heard his own private personal meanings, many things happen. . . . He feels released. . . . He surges forth in a new sense of freedom. I think he becomes more open to the process of change. (44, p. 223–224)

Competent and empathetic listening is perhaps the most basic and most necessary condition for facilitating the development of an open and trusting relationship and for assisting students to achieve more constructive levels of behaving.

Unfortunately, this kind of listening does not pervade each classroom or even most of them. Often a teacher engages in selective listening, hearing only what he wants to hear—those meanings that are least threatening to him. When he cannot avoid hearing messages that are threatening, he frequently twists what the student is saying, distorting the student's real meaning. What the student all too often experiences in the classroom is a teacher's response to a question he never asked. The teacher denies or distorts what the student is really saying, and he does this primarily because he feels that he cannot respond to the student honestly and still remain comfortable with his own feelings.

When the student's initial efforts at communicating his meanings are met with denial or distortion, he reacts with a feeling of frustration, "You are not listening to what I'm trying to say!" When this occurs continually in the classroom, the student gradually comes to believe that honest communication is really impossible.

A suggestion that may help a prospective teacher improve his skills for accurate and sensitive listening has been offered by Carl Rogers. A group of students first selects an issue which is controversial in nature. The students then proceed to engage in a discussion of their attitudes and feelings on the issue with one condition. Before a student may express his own personal views or make a statement, he must restate the meanings that the preceding speaker communicated, and he must restate them to the satisfaction of that speaker. This experiment requires a student to look at his own ability to listen accurately to another person. The student may find that he is unwilling and/or unable to listen to the individual meanings of another person—a shortcoming which suggests that teaching may not be for him. (43)

Accepting. To have a trusting relationship develop between a student and a teacher, there needs to take place acceptance of the student and his expressions of himself, as well as accurate and sensitive listening. The student needs to believe that when he communicates his true feelings and convictions, he will not be criticized for being himself. This assumption has two very important implicatons for classroom teachers. First, teachers may not impose their adult values on students. In many classrooms, children are asked to measure up to adult standards—guidelines which have in some instances no validity even for adults. When children are required and coerced to adapt to adult standards, freedom to communicate one's real self is precluded. Second, when we consider the notion of acceptance we need to distinguish between understanding a person's behavior and approving of it. In accepting a student's behavior we are saying, "I understand, I can see why you feel this way and why you did what you did." The teacher must realize that if a child is to feel accepted, he needs to believe that his behavior is understood.

However, *understanding* the student's present way of coping *is not approving* of it. Approving of behaviors is saying not only, "I understood," but, "it's okay, go ahead." Behavior which is dishonest, destructive or unjust quite clearly needs to be disapproved. When disapproval of behavior is expressed, however, it must be borne in mind that the effectiveness of the teacher's disapproval and the likelihood of a constructive change in the student's behavior are contingent on a climate conducive to a safe examination of the student's behavior and on his ability to display acceptable alternative behaviors. We cannot simply tell the child his behavior is not approved. Alternative behaviors that the child is capable of exhibiting must be identified, and those that are acceptable to both the student and teacher need to be encouraged and rewarded.

To summarize, we must appreciate the importance of accepting a student as a person and distinguishing between understanding his behavior and approving of it. This distinction is essential in attitude and in practice if open and honest inquiry is to take place and if students are to be given the opportunity to undergo constructive changes in their behavior. Accepting a student for himself means appreciating his goals, his methods of achieving goals, his judgment as to whether or not he is successful in his efforts, his fear of a new and different task, his noisy expressions of joy and satisfaction on completing a meaningful project, and his frustrations and anger when he is disappointed with the outcome of a planned activity. If the teacher cannot appreciate the student's behavior and the logic he presents to defend it, the teacher cannot facilitate the student's learning and development. The very process of learning necessarily involves imperfect performance. The teacher who cannot accept the fact that errors are a natural part of learning and developing cannot hope to create a climate of openness and trust and cannot hope to provide conditions appropriate for each student to develop the best that is in him.

He is skilled in the use of different diagnostic, planning, facilitative and evaluative procedures and is knowledgable about their limitations

There are four procedural areas in which the competent teacher is skilled. The competent teacher is first skilled in devising and using tools to diagnose a student's predispositions to learn. He is aware of the strengths and limitations of tools such as achievement tests and intelligence tests, and he is competent in observing, interviewing and in devising pretests and diagnostic questionnaires.

The second skill area is that of planning and coordinating appropriate learning opportunities. He is knowledgeable about available resources; he can identify problems and issues; and he can devise units of study and activities consonant with a student's learning predispositions.

The competent teacher is also skilled in the use of the most appropriate procedures and processes for helping a student achieve particular goals. He is prepared to encourage a student's investigation of problems and issues and to facilitate his completion of activities and tasks.

Finally, a competent teacher is skilled in evaluating. He can identify appropriate achievement criteria that can be used to gauge accurately a student's performance in the activities and tasks planned for him. He can construct and use a number of different types of assessment techniques which incorporate appropriate achievement criteria. He can employ several tools, e. g., objective tests, essay tests, projects, term papers, experiments, and observations, to sample adequately the range of a student's learning. In so doing, he can also assess his own performance and the extent to which he accurately diagnosed a student's learning predispositions and provided approximately for his learning.

Of the four groups of skills that the teacher needs, perhaps the most inadequately developed are those needed to diagnose completely the kinds of learning conditions that each student needs. Traditionally, the diagnostic skills that the teacher develops are those used to identify the deficiencies in the student. The student is then provided with remedial instruction in an effort to have him perform more in line with the norm. As a consequence, the schools avoid facing the real issue—that the true function of diagnosis is to *accept the student where he is* and then determine the most appropriate conditions for him to learn and develop.

The schools need to ask and find answers to such questions as, "What are the different kinds of knowledge that this student now possesses which have a bearing on the subject matter that will be investigated?" "What does he believe the major issues to be?" "What are his ambitions, concerns and values?" "What is his style of learning, and which conditions may be most appropriate for promoting his particular style?" "What kind of psychological climate is necessary for him to function on his own terms?" *The schools must face up to the fact that there is no educational norm; there are only people, each of whom is different, and the schools need to identify these differences and provide learning opportunities accordingly.*

When we say a teacher needs to be skilled in the use of different diagnostic, coordinating, facilitative and evaluative procedures and that he needs to be knowledgeable about their limitations, we are saying that the teacher needs to be *flexible* in the selection and use of available tools, climates, activities and people.

> By far the single most repeated adjective used to describe good teachers is "flexibility." Either implicitly or explicitly (more often the latter), this characteristic emerges time and again over all others when good teaching is discussed in the research. (16, p. 343)

When flexibility characterizes a person's teaching style, he is acutely aware of the appropriateness, value and shortcomings of available procedures and tools. For example, the teacher is aware that . . .

> I.Q. is useful primarily in providing information concerning some of the very basic skills needed to perform at the minimum acceptable academic level in a middle-class school setting.

> I.Q. does not give any *whys* or *hows* regarding the nature of the different kinds of human performances or abilities, but only suggests *what amounts* of the *tested* abilities a given individual exhibited at the time he was tested.

> It is *possible* for a change of as much as 50 I.Q. points to occur during the school year.

> I.Q. accounts for only a small or modest portion of the individual differences in ability to master particular academic subjects.

In short, although the teacher is aware that while I.Q. provides a considerable amount of accurate and useful information concerning many of the individual student's current intellectual abilities, *I.Q. cannot provide accurate information concerning the particular kinds of intellectual predispositions needed to perform successfully in each subject area.*

The teacher is also aware that . . .

pretests, if competently devised, can yield more accurately information about a student's current intellectual skills than either I.Q. or achievement test scores.

pretest scores can be misleading when students suffer from test anxiety.

makers of pretests cannot presume to know and assess *all* of the prerequisite skills and levels of learning that contribute to successful performance in a given subject-matter area.

no pretest can tap all of the significant motivational predispositions and response styles that characterize each student and markedly affect his behavior in new situations.

skilled observation of free and open interaction between students is a valuable *supplementary* tool for identifying students' predispositions to learn.

the cumulative record may provide some useful information concerning a student's physical condition, ambitions and concerns.

the cumulative record is the single most prejudical and destructive diagnostic tool available to the teacher when it is used to "find out what the student can do" and more importantly *"why."*

Concerning individual differences the teacher is aware that . . .

children who are highly anxious and/or highly compulsive perform at higher levels in structured environments than in unstructures ones.

dependent-prone students require more approval, encouragement, and emotional support than less dependent-prone students.

some students are intellectually *impulsive* (immediately respond to an instructor's inquiry) while others tend to be reflective (tend to think things through carefully before responding).

impulsive children tend to commit more errors in reading and in inductive reasoning than children who are reflective.

the traditional kinds of timed classroom tests and grading procedures fail to disclose accurately the performance capabilities of impulsive students and students who are highly reflective in forming their answers to questions.

for some students the *content* of a teacher's judgment is more important that the manner in which it is given, whereas for other students the latter is more important.

Concerning learning outcomes the teacher is aware that . . .

competently utilized programmed materials and technological devices are at least as effective as teachers in dispensing information and stating relationships among concepts.

competently devised nondirective and inquiry-centered classes facilitate greater changes in attitudes, values and generalizable concepts than lecture-type classes, or information dispensing approaches.

logical, convergent or analytical thinking is a necessary condition for solving most problems.

divergent and intuitive thinking are ways of "seeing" problems and solutions that escape the methods of logic.

grouping by true rate of learning is useful for having each student move through a sequence of information within the same period of time.

"homogeneous" grouping is disadvantageous if the goal is to assist students in acquiring and/or changing attitudes, values and generalizable concepts.

I don't believe that I need to go any further to make the point that a competent teacher is fully aware that a single approach to teaching is inadequate for encouraging different kinds of learning in each student. He does not rely on a single diagnostic tool, facilitative process or set of activities and materials to meet the varied needs of his students. Instead, he provides the amounts and kinds of freedom, structure, help, support and guidance that are most appropriate for the goals and individual students in question. To summarize, a competent teacher is more than the traditional kind of subject specialist; he is able to identify, organize and make available for each student the most appropriate kinds of learning resources—activities, equipment, materials, and people. He is informed, sensitive and skilled enough to identify what is appropriate for a particular child in a given situation and to provide it.

He is experimental in his general attitude toward identifying and providing appropriate learning conditions

While the teacher's task is that of providing the learning conditions most appropriate for each person to set and achieve goals that are personally and socially constructive, in many instances he has no way of knowing in advance the particular approaches that will be effective. This suggests that one of the roles of a competent teacher is that of a person who actively and continually inquires into the defensibility of his decisions and practices. He views each decision as an hypothesis that the climate, goals, materials, processes and evaluative procedures he is providing are conducive to the learning and development of each student. An hypothesis is an if-then statement, "if the available information is accurate concerning both the student's learning predispositions and the general effects of particular teaching procedures, then these practices will be appropriate for facilitating this student's learning and development." He continually looks at the quality and quantity of learning that students demonstrate as the evidence which either supports or fails to support his hypothesis.

If the teacher is to be effective in providing learning conditions, he really has no choice but to experiment. The teacher who is afraid to propose and test new approaches becomes an invalid. He relies on coercive techniques, and the truisms of the education culture become his crutches.

A most important issue for the prospective teacher involves his willingness to engage in experimentation. He needs to answer honestly questions such as, "Am I willing to strike out on my own and formulate and test my own hypotheses about appropriate learning conditions?" "Am I willing to run the risk of being criticized by administrators?" "Am I willing to propose and fight for adoption of constructive school policies, policies which may be at odds with existing ones?" These last questions are perhaps the more important ones. The teacher who is innovative will challenge the "right" way handed down by the administration. In most instances the teacher who tries to provide appropriate learning conditions for his students, quite honestly will be trying to bring about a change in school policy.

He can look at his own beliefs, feelings and behavior openly and can find ways to make them more constructive to himself and others

It was noted in Chapter 2 that the teacher makes decisions and utilizes strategies primarily on the basis of his perceptions of students' behaviors and his notion of the role of the teacher. We also know that for a teacher to propose and test hypotheses about appropriate learning conditions and to facilitate the development of constructive behaviors in his students, he needs to have accurate perceptions of himself and of his students.

Perception of Student's Behavior. What are constructive attitudes and behaviors that a competent teacher has toward students? Some evidence suggests the following:

1. He views and treats students as people with unique problems, concerns and points of reference.

2. He values the perception of students—their ways of seeing and interpreting reality.

3. He views and treats students as trustworthy—well intentioned and capable of developing in personally and socially advantageous ways. (4, 44)

Perhaps the single most important belief that a teacher has about students is whether or not students are trustworthy and capable of developing the best that is in them. A teacher who believes that students do not have these characteristics, or that they exist in a way which requires continual management, will adopt strategies which prevent the student from engaging in self-directed learning. However, as we have discussed in previous chapters, such a view of human behavior is extremely difficult to defend. Not only does it fail to receive support from the available evidence, but it is untenable from a practical point of view. We can justify careful management of an infant's behavior because of his relatively low capacity to engage in unsupervised activities without injuring himself. However, as the child learns and develops he requires less and less supervision of his behavior. He increasingly acquires the capacities to engage in self-directed learning that is not injurious to himself and others, and adults become increasingly less able to control the growing child's activities and behavior. Removing scissors from a baby is one thing, but removing drugs from an adolescent is another. *As the child grows older, it becomes increasingly imperative, both to himself and to society, that he develop the capacity to exhibit constructive forms of behavior with the minimum of supervision.*

When we apply this to the school we are saying that each student needs to acquire the capabilities to examine and change his behavior *on his own.* This requires the utilization of teachers who are sensitive to the conditions each student needs to engage in self-directed change. The sensitivity required is more than the skill needed to perceive and record a student's external behavior; it is the capacity to see how the student views himself and his reality.

To acquire accurate perceptions about a student we need to know more about him than simply the physical movements he exhibits in a controlled setting. We need information about his perceptions—his feelings about his classmates, his teachers, the subject matter and himself. If we value people over things, self-directiveness over dependency, and if we are to identify accurately each person's predispositions to engage in self-directed learning, then we need to value the *student's* perceptions of himself as much as we value *our* perceptions of him. This assumption is supported by the evidence that accurate perceptions of a student are most likely to be acquired when observations of his behavior are discussed with other observers and with the student himself. Teachers need to utilize inquiry and discussion approaches to identify a student's relevant learning predispositions, to set advantageous goals, and to facilitate a student's achievement of goals.

Perception of Self.   What are constructive attitudes, beliefs and feelings that teachers have about themselves? Evidence suggests that a competent teacher tends to exhibit the following:

1. *He identifies with other people.* He sees himself as one with other people—happy when they are happy, sad when they are sad, concerned when they are concerned. He feels one with the human condition.

2. *He sees himself as being competent to cope with life's challenges and problems.* He believes that he is capable of accepting each phase of living, of rolling with the punches. He does not view himself as having major failings.

3. *He sees himself as being accepted, needed and wanted by others.* He believes that his judgment and skills are valued and that others see him as being a worthy person.

4. *He can look at himself honestly—see himself with a minimum of distortion and defensiveness.* He is able to confront his feelings and behavior. He can ask himself why he feels and behaves the way he does. For example, he has the capacity to seek honest answers to questions such as, "Why did I feel threatened by today's class discussion?" "Why did I criticize the student who disagreed with me?" "Why did I become angry with students who did not participate actively in class?" The capacity of the teacher to look at himself openly and honestly is among the most important response capabilities that a competent teacher has. (4, 44)

How aware are *you* of the motives and reasons for your behavior? Would you like to participate in an experiment that may help you get some insight into your own attitudes and behavior? If so, try the following proposal. After a discussion class take a sheet of paper and draw a line on it, dividing it into two columns, a "positive" column and a "negative" column. Next write down the qualities that you believe characterize a particular student in your class. Place these perceptions in the appropriate column. Now ask yourself why you believe you perceived the student the way you did. Perhaps it would be helpful if you checked the number of times you used value-laden terms such as good, bad, right, wrong, intelligent, dull. Why do you believe you chose these terms? To what degree do your interests, motives and values influence you to be positive or negative in your judgment about him? Ask yourself to what extent your approval or disapproval, acceptance or rejection of the student's behavior is based on your need to use your own personality as a model or example. Do you generally have positive perceptions of him when his attitudes and behavior are similar to yours? The basic question is, "Do you believe you are capable of seeing each student as unique, entitled to the concerns, feelings and behaviors that are of value to him?" (40)

It may be inferred from the foregoing experiment that if you find it extremely difficult to perceive the reality that the student sees and to become aware of your true feelings and attitudes toward him, then the transactions that will take place in your classroom most likely will not be very meaningful either to you or to your students. This leads us to one of the most important questions that you need to ask yourself, and one which you need to answer openly and honestly. "Why do you want to become a teacher?" or, if it applies, "Why are you now a teacher?" Are your major reasons long vacations and a need to have others see things the way you see them? If among your major reasons for becoming a teacher there is neither a desire to work with the young and to facilitate their development nor to work for the development of a more humane society, do you honestly believe you should consider teaching?

SUMMARY

When we look at the characteristics of successful teachers we find at least four areas of competency: 1) the capacity to create a psychological climate for learning; 2) the ability to identify, plan, provide and assess appropriate learning opportunities; 3) the ability and willingness to experiment and to discover more advantageous approaches to teaching and learning; and 4) the capacity to understand and constructively employ their own behavior.

It should be clear that a teacher must be competent in each of the four areas noted above if he is to help students acquire the necessary skills for a meaningful life. I also suspect that the competencies in areas 1, 3 and 4 are prerequisites for competency in area 2. Consequently, most teachers fail to achieve total competency because they (and perhaps their trainers) believe that competency in area 2 can be acquired in the absence of competencies in areas 1, 3, and 4.

In many instances the teacher's inability to demonstrate competencies in each of the aforementioned areas can be traced to demands made by the school which prevent him from doing an effective job. However, the problem can lie with the teacher-training institutions; many teachers enter classrooms without the necessary skill to promote constructive learning. It is these two issues—the need to reduce the school demands placed on teachers and the need for more effective teacher-training programs —which we will examine in our final chapter.

IMPROVING THE

In most of our schools, conditions are such that teachers need to possess superhuman qualities to do an effective job. In the average public elementary school classroom the teacher is expected to provide appropriate learning conditions for 30 or more students who differ markedly from each other in I.Q. reading level, reasoning ability, motivational states, personal and family problems, physical health and emotional adjustment, and he is expected to have each of these students interested, enthusiastic and successful in all of the activities in which he is involved. In a typical self-contained elementary classroom, the teacher is expected to provide appropriate learning conditions for students who range in I.Q. from 85 to 160. He must have a substantial command of many subject areas— art, English, geography, history, mathematics, music and science; he is expected to have the skills to diagnosis emotional problems and physical illnesses and administer to a whole host of physical and psychological needs. The teacher's job in the typical high school may be a more demanding one. Although he is required to be a subject specialist in only one or two areas, he has at least 100 different students instead of the 30 most elementary teachers have.

In addition, the teacher may need to be a housekeeper, money collector, procurer of materials and disciplinarian. He is required to help

COMPETENCY OF TEACHERS

plan the general school curriculum, extra-curricular activities, school-community events, plays, exhibitions and special occasions; he is expected to demonstrate good citizenship by his involvement in community affairs; he is expected to attend conventions, workshops, conferences, seminars and in-service programs; he is expected to be competent in dealing with all kinds of parents; and he is expected to take the place of parents while each student is in his charge. This means, that with respect to each of her children, the elementary school teacher . . .

> is responsible for his physical and emotional well-being; she must protect him from accidents; know where he is at all times; guard him against older or bigger children, toughs, and intruders; observe his health and take steps if he appears ill; keep an eye on his property; and if he is younger, "mother" him, help him on with his overshoes, and instruct and assist him in the more elementary forms of sanitation. (17, p. 78)

Although the new teacher comes to school idealistic, energetic and enthusiastic, he soon realizes that the more concerned he becomes about students' needs and problems, the more problems he creates for himself, the greater frustration he experiences and the more impossible his job seems to become. When he comes face to face with impossible demands, he resorts to coping strategies. He makes them a permanent part of his repertoire and opposes any suggestions or recommendations for change that would loosen his hold on his survival techniques.

What are the strategies that he adopts? He hangs on to old content and processes, and he concentrates less and less of his efforts on *individual* students. The teacher utilizes procedures that control and manipulate students as a *group*—lecturing, group assignments and mass testing—in order to make less work and create fewer problems for himself. It is easiest for him to lecture to students, test them as one, and then herd them off to someone else. Many students, of course, object to this type of "educational" experience. However, their objections are generally countered by the predictable and often destructive behavior of school personnel.

When the student becomes less and less willing to be manipulated, school officials accuse him of being unruly. To get the student to comply they often set up illogical rules with punishments for violation. When the usual strategies fail to elicit compliance, we either set up discipline rooms or a Learning Center for Disruptive Students, or we remove students from the schools. Even in the "learning centers," the student must comply or he is finished. The position of the school superintendent may well be, "We won't tolerate the student who can't discipline himself." The school demands that a child comply to its ways or he will be dealt with for not disciplining himself. *Self*-discipline becomes conformity to the demands of *other* people. How dishonest and tragic! The damage that this does to students is enormous: satisfactory reading and thinking levels are not achieved; students' curiosity to learn in an educational sense is seriously impaired; students may see themselves as incompetent and worthless, consequently becoming so discouraged or angry that they come to hate school.

What is a reasonable solution to the teacher's impossible task? We need to redefine the school's purpose; we need to adopt a philosophy of teaching and learning which starts and ends with the individuality of the learner; we need to redefine the teacher's job and reform teacher-training programs. The first two of these four recommendations were dealt with in preceding chapters. In the remainder of this chapter we will redefine and reform the teacher's job and teacher-training programs.

REDEFINING THE TEACHER'S JOB

We cannot expect a teacher to be a minor god. He must be provided with tasks that can be performed adequately by one person within a reasonable period of time. The functions that the teacher currently performs must be divided into teaching and nonteaching categories and assigned to people having the appropriate skills. Hart (17) points out that we expect a person to teach the way we once found a cobbler making a pair of boots. He carried out every step of the bootmaking process himself, and he did it all by hand. With the exception of the teacher, no professional or specialist is asked to perform the functions of other specialists. The campus security officers are not asked to operate and maintain the school's heating system and vice versa. In hospitals we do not find a class of patients in the charge of each doctor, who is required to perform *all* of the necessary functions to serve *each* patient—from taking temperatures through performing surgery. If we did require the doctor to perform all of the medical services, the quality of care each patient received would be approximately equal to the learning conditions each student receives in a classroom—*poor*! Although the regular changing of beds and taking of temperatures are necessary functions in a hospital, we would not take the cardiologist or neurosurgeon away from other duties to perform these tasks.

We need to have differentiated roles in teaching so teachers are not taken away from their most important duties—those of identifying and providing the best conditions for each student to learn. All other tasks and functions should be assumed by personnel with appropriate skills. We need to establish several levels of ascending skill with specific and specialized functions and responsibilities at each level. We must have teacher's aides and paraprofessionals perform essentially nonteaching functions, allowing teachers to assume only a teaching role. We must replace guidance counselors and school psychologists with school learning specialists who are intimately involved in the educational process. (I'm sure that the groans of counselors and psychologists to this proposal will be loud and clear.)

However, we must face the fact that the overwhelming majority of our school psychologists and guidance counselors are presently being trained to perform functions which are largely divorced from the continuous process of learning and development that the student experiences. For example, the school psychologist in most schools is only remotely involved in assisting students and teachers. He generally visits a school one or two days a week, and then he usually looks at the behavior of only problem students. He gives these students one or more psychological tests and compares their scores with the national norms. Then his findings are matched with a category devised by psychologists to explain why the students behave the way they do in school. Each student is given a psychological label, e.g., "underachiever," which relieves the school of its responsibility for viewing each student as having his own norm and needing separate conditions to perform on his own terms.

The function of the guidance counselor is even more disturbing. In most cases he is grossly incompetent to counsel students who have *personal* problems. He is used by the schools primarily to test–and–place students, and to help students "understand" teachers and the school's "socializing" function. The guidance counselor's role and effectiveness in the area of *vocational* counseling is not much different. All too often the students who are most in need of guidance are least likely to receive it. For example, counseling at the high school level is devoted largely to the youths who plan to go to college. While college bound students need counseling, students who are not heading for college and the students who are the predictable dropouts receive little, if any, guidance in deciding what they want to and *can* do when they leave school. Unfortunately, in many schools, the most important function assigned to the guidance counselor is that of helping the principal run a smoothly operating machine.

The guidance counselor and, to an even greater extent, the school psychologist are used by the school primarily to convey the impression that the schools are concerned about the personal development of each student. In reality, however, neither has any prolonged involvement with the process of a student's learning and development. The guidance counselor and school psychologist must be replaced by specialists who will continually work with the classroom teacher in assisting each student to learn and develop. Advisement, counseling and the writing of recommendations for college, trade school or a job must be performed only by persons who are continually involved in identifying and providing appropriate learning conditions for each student. They alone would be qualified to make judgments about the performance capabilities of students.

How can we insure more competent teaching and effective learning? I propose that in each school the job of identifying and providing the most appropriate conditions for each student to learn would be assumed by *five levels* of teachers and school learning specialists. Each level of competency would require different degrees of specialization in four skill categories, which are: 1) *diagnosing* students' needs and current levels of functioning, 2) *planning* and *coordinating* subject matter with learning activities and materials, 3) *facilitating* goal achievement through a variety of processes, and 4) *evaluating* students' achievement and the appropriateness of the learning conditions provided. The Level I professional, the teacher, would receive basic training in each skill category. Mastery of the requirements for Level I would be a prerequisite for advancement. Level II would require specialization in one of the four basic skills, and each successive level would require an additional specialized skill. A year of course work and internship would be necessary for each category of specialization. It must be borne in mind that the teacher's competency in each of these four skill areas is contingent (as noted in the preceding chapter) on: a) his capacity to create a psychologically safe environment for the learner, b) his ability and willingness to experiment and c) his capacity to understand and constructively employ his own behavior.

Every school would have a corp of school learning specialists, who would be located in the school's Learning Resources Center, and they would work closely with each teacher to provide students with appropriate learning conditions. They would also be responsible for holding periodic conferences and seminars with each teacher to discuss the strengths and limitations of available equipment, procedures and materials for promoting learning.

In summary, when we consider the task of redefining the teacher's role, we need to identify duties and responsibilities at a number of levels. The teacher would be responsible for individualizing learning conditions for each student. School learning specialists would be intimately involved in assisting teachers to identify and provide the most appropriate conditions for each student to learn in personally and socially advantageous ways.

REFORM IN TEACHER TRAINING

If the schools are to have competent teachers and school learning specialists, basic reform in teacher education must accompany the redefining of the teacher's functions. The overwhelming majority of teacher-training programs in our colleges and universities require trainees to go through experiences that are irrelevant to the individual trainee's needs and to the kinds of learning conditions that need to be provided in the schools.

Virtually all colleges of education carry programs that serve only to perpetuate the appalling conditions found in the public schools. The personnel responsible for teacher–training programs are in many cases opposed to substantive change. When educators do speak of progress, they often want to undertake a patchwork approach or merely jazz up the existing system to bring about in a more efficient manner essentially the same results. Thus, behavior modification, programmed instruction, microteaching, and computer-assisted instruction are viewed as ways of "changing" current learning and teaching conditions. While these techniques may be quite serviceable in some phases of learning and teaching, the basic issue which needs to be faced is that fundamental changes are needed in the prevailing philosophy of teaching, in the entire structure of courses and experiences for trainees, and in the teaching models found in teacher–training centers. If teacher trainers are unwilling to make the necessary changes in *their own behavior* and in the kinds of learning conditions they make available to trainees, they cannot blame our public school teachers for being incompetent, inflexible or out–of–date in their practices.

Personnel who are responsible for teacher-training programs also need to take a long hard look at what's going on in the different kinds of public schools. For too long most of our leaders of education have been unwilling to acknowledge the pervasiveness of the unsatisfactory learning and teaching conditions in the public schools. For example, Dr. Robert Havighurst, a distinguished professor at the University of Chicago, maintains that the students who are performing poorly in our public schools constitute only about 15 per cent of the total school population. "The other 85 per cent of American children," he says, "are doing quite well in school." He maintains that the children who are doing poorly in school are the "socially disadvantaged." He attacks critics such as Paul Goodman, Edgar Friedenberg, Nat Hentoff, John Holt, Herbert Kohl, and Jonathan Kozol. He calls them "anarchists" because they are critical of existing rules and institutions. He accuses them of "agonizing in public over their discovery that the world is a difficult place." (18, pp. 20–21) I find Professor Havighurst's views of the public schools and their critics very unsettling. It is terribly unfair to consider anyone who criticizes the appalling conditions in many of our public schools an anarchist or public cry-baby. We need not agree with all of the indictments of the public schools, nor need we support all of the proposals for change that the school critics make, however, we do need to look hard at their observations, assumptions and conclusions. The crisis in education pervades every city and state in America. Goodlad (13) doubts that the schools serve even 50 per cent of their clientele in reasonably satisfying ways. Although poor teaching and learning conditions are evident in schools at all socieconomic levels, many educational leaders only see problems for the financially poor or socially disadvantaged. This kind of selective data processing is in large part responsible for the poor training that colleges of education provide for prospective teachers.

Schools of education are careful not to provide students with an opportunity to examine openly and honestly the current public school conditions and the plight of students and teachers alike. In many teacher-training programs students do not see a classroom of students until their senior year when they do their student teaching. Each semester a large number of seniors are shocked when they go out into the schools for the first time. Their confrontation with the realities of the public schools (one that should have been provided no later than the sophomore year) convinces many that teaching is not for them. These students cannot retrieve the three and a half years spent in the teacher–training program, nor can they change their major. *No, students do not "fail." The process fails.* It fails to provide students with the experiences they need to make an informed choice very early in their college career. It is clear that until educational institutions honestly examine the conditions that exist in our public schools and address themselves to basic changes in their philosophies of learning and teaching and in their structure of a training program and education curriculum, the unsatisfactory conditions currently existing in the public schools will remain. Large numbers of unskilled and/or disillusioned people go into teaching, and they do so because schools of education are more concerned about efficiency and the status quo than they are about the quality of teachers they send into the public schools.

A Basic Program

The content in most teacher-training programs consist largely of theory that is vaguely related to the realities of teaching. With few exceptions, opportunities for trainees to work with students in actual classrooms are limited to a process called *student teaching,* which is not training, but a feeble trial and error experiment and screening device.

What are some of the basic preparatory experiences all teachers should have? Throughout the entire teacher-training program each trainee needs to become well informed in the subject areas in which he plans to teach and in the humanities and social sciences. Moreover, when study in the humanities and social sciences is integrated with an examination of the basic issues in education, the trainee is more likely to become aware of the principles and problems of human development, learning and teaching. All of the above goals would be achieved primarily through reading lists, research papers and inquiry sessions, which would be planned by the trainee and his teachers.

To enable the trainee to acquire the technical skills and personal qualities of a competent facilitator of learning, four phases of training would be provided for him. First, each trainee would be provided with opportunities to observe and interact with children and adolescents in different settings *inside and outside* the school environment. At the same time opportunities would be arranged which would require each trainee to identify and examine critically his basic beliefs about himself and others. He would determine if his beliefs serve to promote learning in others, or if changes in his beliefs about himself and others are needed and possible. (This self-evaluation would take place not only at the beginning of the student's training, but during each of the remaining phases of the program.)

The second phase of preparation would combine the study of available *diagnostic, planning, facilitative* and *evaluative* procedures with opportunities to observe them and assist in their utilization in actual classroom practice. Trainees would assist competent facilitators of learning in a) *identifying* the individual student's current rate and style of learning, b) *planning* a variety of activities and conditions appropriate for students' different rates and styles of learning, c) *initiating* and *guiding* activities which enable students to achieve the planned goals, and d) *evaluating* students' achievement of planned objectives and their own effectiveness as a facilitator of learning.

The third phase would be a period of internship, during which time the trainee would apply his constructive attitudes and skills to individualizing learning conditions for each student. He would work first with a very small number of students, perhaps only one. The opportunity to identify and provide appropriate learning conditions for only one or two students initially would increase the trainee's chance of developing the competencies needed to become a successful teacher. After the trainee could work successfully with one or two students, he would work with progressively larger groups until he could work successfully with a group of 30 students at one time. The intership would not be "student teaching" but *training* in an environment which would provide appropriate learning conditions for the trainee and comprehensive feedback and assessment of his behavior. In short, the trainee would be provided with the conditions which would enable him to a) *design* programs appropriate for students varying in their rates and styles of learning and in their interests and goals, and b) *redesign* learning conditions and *revise* programs when his assessment of students' learning and his own behavior indicates that modifications are necessary.

After his internship, the trainee would complete his final phase of training, a year of teaching in the public schools experiencing the full range of duties and responsibilities involved in being a teacher. Hopefully, he would have the title of *Teacher* and would be granted the freedom to employ any constructive teaching approach he considered appropriate.

If the trainee wished to become a school learning specialist, he would enter advanced training sessions and do additional internship to develop the advanced performance capabilities needed in one or more of the four skill categories.

It is important to note that the supervision of a trainee's teaching or field experiences *should not* be assumed by persons who have not worked with the trainee in *course and laboratory* experiences. All too often field supervisors are unaware of the kinds of knowledge and skills trainees acquire in their pre-field experiences. Consequently, in many instances, the supervisors' competencies and behavior are in substantial conflict with the beliefs and performance capabilities, which trainees take into the field. In other instances, supervsors are simply *less knowledgeable and competent* than the trainees themselves. Clearly, both tasks—the direction of course and laboratory experiences and the direction of field experiences—need to be assumed to a large extent by the same persons. This becomes especially important when we consider the effect supervisors have on the trainee's actual classroom performance. The supervisor, more than any other person in a teacher-training program, is being counted on by the trainee to support him in the public school classroom as he attempts to develop his own individual teaching style.

An equally important issue is that teacher trainers need to make reality checks at regular intervals. *All* persons directly connected with the training of teachers should be required to return to the public school classroom every two or three years and teach a full semester to keep in touch with the conditions and realities of the public schools and to appreciate the kinds of experiences their trainees are having in the classroom.

Individual Differences in Trainees

It must be borne in mind that individual differences exist in trainees just as they do in the children they will teach. Some trainees have more constructive attitudes and values toward children than other trainees when they enter the program. Each trainee has his own learning rate and his own style of working with information and people. Consequently, there must be enough flexibility to allow trainees to proceed at different rates in the training program and to develop their own unique constructive teaching strategies.

The issue of individual differences in trainees is important also with respect to screening and certifying teachers. One factor that makes it difficult to settle on selection criteria of trainees is that a number of different teaching strategies are effective in providing appropriate learning conditions. Another problem is that many trainees may develop the necessary skills and attitudes *after* an initial evaluation procedure is used. To deal with these problems, we need to have an *ongoing* evaluation program. Trainees need to receive feedback continually, both from their trainers and the students they teach, to make a judgment as to whether or not they are acquiring the needed competencies within a reasonable amount of time and with a reasonable amount of effort. Trainees need to determine early whether they can acquire the capabilities to diagnose each student's starting points and provide a climate for the open and honest exchanges of ideas.

When criteria are established for evaluating or selecting prospective teachers, two important distinctions must be made. First, we need to distinguish between the trainee's ability to secure high grades in his course work and his ability to provide appropriate learning conditions for a group of students. Therefore, the basic question which needs to be asked is, "Can this trainee demonstrate an effective teaching strategy, i.e., help students to learn and develop in personally satisfying ways?" A student's grade-point average and the number of education courses he completes may be of little consequence when it comes to "cutting it" as a teacher in the classroom. The major implication of this distinction is that the traditional course approach to teacher traning needs to be supplanted by training in environments which simulate the real-life conditions of the public schools. Second, the technology of teaching—the skills needed to utilize a variety of teaching procedures—and the art of teaching—the personal qualities needed to engage others in open and constructive interactions—are two different competencies. A basic conclusion we can draw from available research and clinical evidence about effective teaching is that the trainee may be highly skilled and knowledgeable in the use of diagnostic tools, in planning and organizing subject content and in utilizing technological devices, yet be unable to establish a climate of trust and elicit free and honest communications from students. A teacher can be highly skilled in the use of available learning resources, yet fail to engage students in constructive and meaningful learning because he harbors negative feelings and attitudes toward himself and others. For example, although teachers can be trained to demonstrate the *functional* skills to teach in disadvantaged areas, they may be unsuccessful due to their failure to come to grips with the prejudice in themselves. Mastery of the technical skills needed to teach is a necessary condition for assisting each student to learn and develop in constructive ways, but equally important is assisting the trainee to face his attitudes toward himself and others and the effects they have on the processes of learning and teaching. It is essential, therefore, that prospective teachers develop the competencies necessary to design functionally appropriate learning conditions and to come face to face with personal attitudes.

A FINAL WORD

How do you initiate substantive change in our public schools and in our colleges of education? In seeking educational change, four points are worth noting. First, changes do not come about simply because people *talk* about change. Personal involvement is essential and it is a mistake to wait for leadership from others. People who want change must ally themselves and work as a *group* to initiate change. A second point relates to the question, "For whose benefit are changes to be made?" Substantive changes in the conditions under which teachers work do not necessarily ensure significant improvements in the conditions under which students learn. Higher salaries, smaller student-teacher ratios and a redefining of the teacher's job will certainly improve the teacher's lot; yet students may still be exposed to irrelevant materials and indefensible teaching practices. Moreover, giving the faculty more decision-making power also fails to guarantee attention to the individual needs of students. In fact, as far as the students are concerned, the "tyranny of the administration" may simply be transferred from the principal to the faculty. Consequently, when people seek change they need to determine whether or not the proposed changes will serve to improve *both* teaching and learning conditions.

Another important point to note regarding the initiation of educational reform is that the making of general statements about the broad areas in which changes are needed is not enough. Asking for "better conditions" is a fine starting point; but change cannot come about until the people who want change list the particular conditions which need to be improved and spell out in detail constructive and workable alternatives to the present system.

The final point deals with strategies. Once the defensible and workable alternatives to the present system have been formulated, the people favoring reform must employ the means most *appropriate* to bring about the specific changes proposed. By and large, students and school personnel will be most effective in producing educational reform when they involve themselves in the tactics of political activism, group pressure and salesmanship. Each change-agent must bear in mind, however, that the appropriateness of a specific strategy for change is dependent upon the particular kind of change sought. For example, political activism may be a highly effective approach for bringing about increases in teachers' salaries, yet be ineffective for changing a school's curriculum.

In summary, when people *want* educational change, they need to a) ally themselves, b) identify the specific purposes for which they are seeking change, c) define in workable terms the specific changes they want, and d) outline and implement the strategies that are most appropriate for the goals to be achieved.

REFERENCES

1. Bowers, W. J. "Student Study Shows College Cheating High," *Columbus Dispatch,* Columbus, Ohio, January 24, 1965.
2. Carlson, S., and Wegner, K. W. "College Dropout," *Phi Delta Kappan,* March 1965.
3. Combs, A. W. (editor). *Perceiving, Behaving, Becoming: A New Focus For Education,* 1962 ASCD Yearbook, Washington, D. C.: Association for Supervision and Curriculum Development, 1962.
4. Combs, A. W. *The Professional Education of Teachers,* Boston: Allyn and Bacon, Inc., 1965.
5. Crary, R. W. *Humanizing The School: Curriculum Development And Theory.* New York: Alfred A. Knopp, 1969.
6. Fantini, M. D., and Weinstein, G. *The Disadvantaged: Challenge to Education.* New York: Harper & Row, 1968.
7. Fitzsimmons, S. J., et al. "School Failures; Now and Tomorrow," *Developmental Psychology,* I, ii (1969), 134–146.
8. Friedenberg, E. Z. *The Dignity of Youth and Other Atavisms,* Boston: Beacon Press, 1965.
9. Friedenberg, E. Z. "An Ideology of School Withdrawal," *Profile of the School Dropout.* Edited by D. Schreiber, New York: Vintage Books, 1968.
10. Fromm, Erich. *Man for Himself,* Greenwich, Conn.: Fawcett, 1965.
11. Gale, R. F. *Developmental Behavior: A Humanistic Approach.* New York: The Macmillan Company, 1969.
12. Goodlad, J. I. "Some Effects of Promotion and Nonpromotion Upon the Social and Personal Adjustment of Children," *Journal of Experimental Education,* XXII (June 1954), 301–328.
13. Goodlad, J. I. "The Schools vs. Education," *Saturday Review,* April 19, 1969.
14. Goodlad, J. I., and Anderson, R. H. *The Nongraded Elementary School.* New York: Harcourt, Brace and World, Inc., 1959.
15. Gordon, R., and Gordon, K. *The Blight on the Ivy.* Englewood Cliffs, New Jersey: Prentice-Hall, 1963.

16. Hamachek, D. "Characteristics of Good Teachers and Implications for Teacher Education," *Phi Delta Kappan,* February 1969.
17. Hart, L. A. *The Classroom Disaster.* New York: Teachers College Press, 1969.
18. Havighurst, R. "Requirements for a Valid 'New Criticism'," *Phi Delta Kappan,* September 1968.
19. Holt, J. *How Children Fail.* New York: Pitman, 1967.
20. Huffington, P. W. *Pupil Dropout Study: Maryland Public Schools.* Maryland: State Department of Education, 1962.
21. Jackson, D. "Crack-Ups on the Campus," *Life,* January 8, 1965.
22. Kamii, C. K., and Weikart, D. P. Marks, "Achievement and Intelligence of Seventh Graders Who Were Retained (Nonpromoted) Once in Elementary School," *Journal of Educational Research LVI* ix, (May-June 1963), 452–459.
23. Kennedy, R. F. et al. "Ghetto Education," *The Center Magazine.* Santa Barbara: Center for the Study of Democratic Institutions, November 1968.
24. Kohl, H. *36 Children.* New York: New American Library, 1967.
25. Kozol, J. *Death at an Early Age.* Boston: Houghton Mifflin, 1967.
26. Leacock, E. B. *Teaching and Learning in City Schools: A Comparative Study.* New York: Basic Books, Inc., 1969.
27. Lembo, J. M. *The Psychology of Effective Classroom Instruction.* Columbus, Ohio: Charles E. Merrill Publishing Co., 1969.
28. Maier, N. R. F. *Problem-Solving Discussions and Conferences: Leadership Methods and Skills.* New York: McGraw-Hill Book Co., 1963.
29. Massialas, B. G., and Zevin, J. *Creative Encounters in the Classroom.* New York: John Wiley & Sons, Inc., 1967.
30. Mercer, B. E., and Carr, E. R. *Education and the Social Order.* New York: Rinehart, 1957.
31. Miller, S. M. "The Search for an Educational Revolution," *Profile of the School Dropout.* Edited by Schreiber, New York: Vintage Books, 1968.
32. Minuchin, P., et. al. *The Psychological Impact of School Experience.* New York: Basic Books, Inc., 1969.
33. *National Enquirer* September 8, 1968.
34. *Newsweek* May 2, 1966.
35. *Newsweek* December 29, 1969.
36. *Newsweek* February 16, 1970.
37. Official statement of The Committee on Academic Freedom, approved by Board of Directors of National Council for the Social Studies. *Social Education,* May 1953.
38. Panel on Educational Research & Development, Innovation and Experimentation on Education. Washington, D.C.: U.S. Government Printing Office, 1964.
39. Perkins, H. "A Procedure for Assessing the Classroom Behavior of Students and Teachers," *American Educational Research Journal,* 1964, 249–260.

40. Postman, N., and Weingartner, G. *Teaching as a Subversive Activity.* New York: Delacorte Press, 1969.

41. Remmers, H. H., and Franklin, R. D. "Sweet Land of Liberty," *Phi Delta Kappan,* XLIV (1962), 22–27.

42. *Report of the National Advisory Commission of Civil Disorders* ("Riot Report"). New York: Bantam Books and The New York Times Co., 1968.

43. Rogers, C. R. *On Becoming a Person.* Boston: Houghton Mifflin Co., 1961.

44. Rogers, C. R. *Freedom to Learn.* Columbus, Ohio: Charles E. Merrill Publishing Co., 1969.

45. Rosenthal, R., and Jacobson, L. F. "Teacher Expectations for the Disadvantaged," *Scientific American,* CCXVIII, iv (1968).

46. Schreiber, D. (editor). *Profile of the School Dropout.* New York: Vintage Books, 1968.

47. Silberman, C. E. "Technology in the Schools," *Readings on the School in Society.* Edited by P. C. Sexton. Englewood Cliffs, New Jersey: Prentice-Hall, 1967

48. Strom, R. D. "Problems of the Successful," *The High School Journal,* LI, iv (April 1968).

49. Strom, R. D. *Psychology for the Classroom.* Englewood Cliffs, New Jersey: Prentice-Hall, 1969.

50. Thomas, S., and Knudsen, D. D. "The Relationship between Nonpromotion and the Dropout Problem," *Theory Into Practice, IV,* iii (June 1965).